INDIAN DRESS

Charles Louis Fabri (1899-1968), Hungarian by birth and British by citizenship, made India his home and devoted much of his life to the advancement of Indian art.

He obtained all his higher education in Holland and was Conservator, Kern Institute of Indian Archaeology, Leyden, when he first visited India in 1931 with Sir Aurel Stein on an archaeological expedition which took him also to Turkey and Iran. He returned in 1934, at the invitation of Rabindranath Tagore, to teach art history at Santiniketan and thereafter became associated with the Archaeological Survey of India. He edited the Survey's *Annual Reports* from 1930-31 to 1933-34, and did field-work at the Mohenjodaro and Takshashila excavations. A great deal of reorganisational work was carried out by him at the Lahore Central Museum, where he was posted as Officer on Special Duty (1936-37), and later as Curator (1946-48).

From 1948 till his death he lived in Delhi writing, lecturing, broadcasting on art and drama. He knew about a dozen languages, European and Asian, and was altogether a most remarkable man. Apart from over two hundred articles and papers, during his lifetime he published five monographs: *Guide to the Stone Age* (1947), *Indian Flamingo* (1947, a novel), *A History of Indian Dress* (1961), *An Introduction to European Painting* (1964). Of the two posthumous publications, *Discovering Indian Sculpture* (1970) and *History of the Art of Orissa* (1974), the latter was published by Orient Longman.

INDIAN DRESS
a brief history

CHARLES FABRI
illustrated by the author

Sangam Books

INDIAN DRESS

Published by
Sangam Books Limited
57 London Fruit Exchange,
Brushfield Street
London E1 6EP, U.K.

First published by Sangam Books Ltd. 1994

By arrangement with
Orient Longman Limited
3-6-272 Himayatnagar
Hyderabad 500 029 (A.P.) India

© Charles Louis Fabri 1960
   Cover design format
© Orient Longman Ltd. 1993

ISBN 0 86311 507 1

Typeset by
Graphic Letters Private Limited
202, Magnum House 1, (opp. Milan Cinema)
Najafgarh Road, New Delhi 110 015

Printed in India by
Rekha Printers Private Limited
A-102/1 Okhla Industrial Area Phase II
New Delhi 110 020

CONTENTS

Publisher's Note vii

I General Introduction 1
II Materials 16
III Milestones 20

List of Plates 27

Abbreviations in References
for Plates 31
Plates I to XXX 32

Bibliography:
I On Costume 93
II Art History 94
III On Painting 95

Index 99

PUBLISHER'S NOTE

When Orient Longman first published *A History of Indian Dress* in 1961, and promoted it as 'one of the few authoritative books ever published on Indian costume', the author protested indignantly in a letter to the publishers: 'This is totally untrue, and I would like you to show me one single authoritative book on Indian Costume, let alone "a few"... The whole point about my books is that it is the first and so far the only authoritative book on the subject and thus a pioneer book'.

The book was reissued in 1977 in a popular paperback edition with a new title *Indian Dress: a brief history*. The text and illustrations remained the same, except for Plates VII, XVI, XIX, XX, XXII and XXIX, which were previously in colour.

In this new edition, the Bibliography and the list of abbreviations in references for the Plates have been rearranged in alphabetical order for ease of reference, and the book has been freshly designed and reset.

The publishers are grateful to Dr Daljit, Keeper of Paintings, National Museum, New Delhi for her immense help in locating and procuring the miniature painting reproduced on the cover.

I. GENERAL INTRODUCTION

The aim of this booklet is threefold.

Dress, as must be obvious to anyone interested in humanity, is a marked characteristic of any culture. Fashions in dress are as interesting to observe as any other facet of human self-expression: the tastes and tendencies of an age are clearly indicated by the type of clothes a period fancies.

Thus, when Indian baroque is in its heyday in other utterances of art—in literature, in sculpture, in painting, in architecture—the same profusion of ornamentation, the same love of dramatic and unusual elements, the same tendency to individualism and romanticism are found in the fashions of the day. (Plates XI, XIV).

Or, to quote another striking example, the fashions at the aristocratic court of the Mughal emperors—and they changed every five or ten years—are typical of a luxury-loving, elegant, sophisticated and close-knit society (Plates XIX, XXI, XXIII, XXV and XXVI).

The second aim of this book is equally important.

Because fashions change, a careful observation of these changes is one of the most powerful tools in the hands of an art historian. For it is possible to date paintings and sculpture within a generation when no other data, such as inscriptions, are available, by an accurate attention to the clothes worn by the human figures depicted.

This method has been used in the West, where detailed histories of costume are available, with excellent results. In India very little such work has been done so far, with the exception of the Mughal period. Considering how uncertain is the dating of Indian art objects, any fresh contribution, however slight, is valuable.

The Mughal period fashions are now so well known that a

miniature can be dated often within five years with no other auxiliary method than that of costume history. One of the most fascinating of human documents is the observation that there are Mughal miniatures in which all the younger courtiers (*darbaris*) are shown in the latest, modish dress, whilst the older gentlemen in the same picture still sport the kind of fashion that was in vogue ten or twenty years earlier. Such devastating realism cannot, of course, be expected of every period, though it is remarkable how accurate the Indian artist was about the minutest detail of costume and jewellery in his own age.

The third aim of a study of historical dress is of a purely practical nature.

It is to help the costume designer for stage and cinema, or the illustrator of history.

The present position is that there is considerable ignorance about dress and habit as it existed in ancient and medieval India. Unfortunately, this ignorance is sometimes coupled with pretence, so that inaccurate and anachronistic productions are claimed as being authentic. Such a misleading of the public can only be halted if reliable information on the history of Indian dress is readily available.

My learned friend Dr Moti Chandra's valuable Hindi book, *Prachin Bharatiya Ves-bhusha* (Allahabad), contains a mass of useful material and 429 figures, but it does not fully serve the three purposes mentioned above. The dating in that book is rather broad. Chapter 8, to mention one example, deals with 'Dress in the Art of Gandhara, Mathura and the South of India', a period that covers over eight hundred years (in the case of Mathura, a thousand). Objects as far removed from each other as fig. 16 (1st century A.D.) and fig. 17 (3rd century B.C.), are treated as contemporary; the *Jataka* tales, written down in their present form in the 4th century A.D., are quoted as evidence for the state of things in the times of the Buddha (5th century B.C.); the attire of divinities and apsarases (heavenly dancing girls) and winged supernatural beings are treated on a par with that of humans; all the paintings at Ajanta are treated as belonging to one era, though they were painted over a period of one thousand years (see Fabri, *Ajanta Frescoes*, in *Marg*, IX, 1); and hardly any distinction is made between the dress of foreigners and Indians. Whilst the book contains much excellent literary evidence and is a valuable and pioneering piece of research, the lack of accurate dating of each illustration robs it of much of its value.

In this book due care has been taken to select examples that are known to represent human, and *not* divine personages. Although the representation of gods and goddess all through Hindu and Buddhist art shows marked reliance on the prevailing fashions in the upper classes—indeed, it has been said that 'Indian gods live like glorified rajas'—yet it was my intention to avoid the slightest ambiguity, and all the pictures that follow are representations of ordinary mortals, the princes and people of India as they lived, and what they wore. *There is not the remotest reason to surmise that the kind of dresses here depicted were not actually worn by the people in those days.*

It is necessary to emphasize this for the simple reason that costume history is completely unknown in India and hence most people, when confronted with the facts, find them difficult to accept. It is difficult to believe for most Indians of today that Indian women of all classes went about bare from the waist upwards (as do the Balinese) for many hundreds of years; neverthless, this is a fact that shouts from thousands and tens of thousands of sculptures and paintings. The evidence is not only overwhelming, it is absolutely conclusive. Anyone with eyes can see that in the whole history of Indian art, from the earliest times to approximately the 12th century A.D., women are invariably shown (with the sole exception of *foreign* fashions at one period) as wearing no garment to cover their breasts.

The suggestion has been made by Indian scholars of today, brought up in very different traditions of propriety and decorum, that this is nothing but an artistic convention. Their argument runs like this: the Greeks also depicted their women in the nude, yet it is not accepted that Greek women went about completely undraped; *ergo*, Indian women must have worn upper garments.

As will be evident to western readers, this argument does

not hold good at all. The Greeks, like many other people, no doubt depicted the nude with relish, but we have thousands of other illustrations of every style of dress worn at various times by all classes of Greeks, men and women. Detailed histories of ancient Greek costume are available, based on thousands of documents. But in ancient Indian art *all* women are always shown with a bare upper body—villagers, townswomen, queens, housewives, milkmaids and the rest. One should certainly not place too much reliance on the representations in Indian art purporting to be counterfeits of supernatural beings: gods, goddesses, godlings, nymphs, dryads and their like.

But is it conceivable that King Mahendravarman would have allowed his two wives to be shown as bare from the waist upwards, if their majesties were in the habit of draping their breasts? Yet we possess a fine sculpture of the king with his two queens, showing them with no more than a single garment falling from the waistline.

Similarly, the lady in my Plate XVII is a 13th century Chola queen, after a bronze image, depicting her as wearing a finely worked lower garment (a *dhoti*) and jewellery: nothing else. It is inconceivable that such a superb portrait would be so utterly divorced from reality that a part of the queen's body which she always covered would be shown here as bare.

At Ajanta we have a vast conglomeration of human figures from horsegrooms to pilgrims, from fishermen to sailors from princes to men-at-arms, from ladies-in-waiting to shopkeepers in the bazaar streets; we have a picture of a sick-nurse about to give first aid to a fainting lady, we have dancing women and musicians at a performance, we watch messengers bringing news, hunters at their nefarious work, idle townswomen looking out of their windows to see what is happening in the street, boatmen at their oars; in fact, men, women and children from every walk of life.

All the upper, and most of the lower class women are shown as wearing no upper garment whatever, unless it be a thin veil-like diaphanous gauze scarf (seen only in a very few pictures in any case). The only women who wear any dress over their upper bodies are foreigners and the maidservants of royalty, and these must also be taken to be foreigners, mostly *yavanikas*. Yazdani has already observed (*Ajanta*, vol. 1, text, p. 9) that it was only maidservants who had 'their breasts properly covered by costumes and materials of various designs.'

Both in Sanskrit drama and in Tamil literature, frequent reference is made to the foreign, 'western' maidservants, especially those who were ladies-in-waiting at court. The word 'Yavanika', though it literally means 'Ionian girl' (*i.e.* Greek), must be taken to mean anyone coming from western Asia, then under the spell of Greek custom and art. (In a similar manner that much later term 'rumi', though literally 'Roman', was used for the whole of Roman-influenced West Asia, especially Syria and Palestine). Even as late as in the play *Mudrarakshasa*, the maid-in-waiting is a Yavanika.

Foreign entertainers, especially dancers and singers, were as welcome in ancient India as they are today. The male dancer in the magnificent mural painting in the Bagh Caves, is a Central Asian, wearing a Scythian cap, high boots, a characteristic Central Asian coat with belt (or sash), and long trousers. The lovely, sinuous dancing girl in the Ajanta cave painting (*Mahajanaka-jataka*) is obviously *completely differently dressed from all the other women in the caves*, for she wears a long-sleeved garment with a plastron in front, probably bare at the back. She is evidently another foreign entertainer. Had there been one (or more) example of this style of long-sleeved plastron-blouse on any woman in any other painting, one would have come to the conclusion that this was, in fact, an Indian fashion; but there is none.

Very rarely, perhaps once in a thousand, one finds a representation of a woman wearing a thinly rolled scarf or a ribbon across the breast, as if to hold up its full, heavy bulbousness. This does not hide the breasts, and cannot be considered a 'covering'. The late Mr Longhurst has pointed out that the Mother Goddess Durga is the only goddess who is frequently shown with this ribbon-like binder. As she is a fertility goddess, the implication is obvious: the breasts are heavy with mother's milk and must be supported.

This discussion has been necessary in order to remove a

wide-spread misunderstanding. The reader is asked to imagine ancient India as another Island of Bali, where no one wore upper garments, except perhaps foreigners. It is pertinent to remark here that even today in some parts of India blouses of any kind are not worn at all. In Kerala, up to the present day, women are seen in the villages with uncovered breasts. In Orissa State the great majority of women, both Oriyas and aborigines, have no breast-covering at all; in many parts of Andhra, blouses are as good as unknown, and even in the towns I have seen many women without more covering than a sari-end thrown casually over one shoulder.

The first recorded examples of the *choli*, the bodice or blouse, are found, to my knowledge, in the pre-Mughal miniature paintings of Gujarat, mostly Jain religious manuscript illuminations. Though a few of these may well go back to the 10th century A.D., the example given in my Plate XVI is dated by Prof. Norman Brown at 1127 A.D. It is the first example in this book of an upper garment for a woman. It covers only the front, the back being bare—a type of blouse that can be found in many areas of Northern India, especially Rajasthan, up to the present day. For another two hundred years or so, sculpture and some of the miniatures occasionally show women with undraped breasts, but the gradual adoption of the *choli* is everywhere evident in Northern India; not, however, in South India, where bodices were not widely worn before the 19th century. It may be interesting to note that the word *choli* seems to come from the word *chola*, 'the body', just as the English 'bodice' comes from 'body'.

There is another fallacious belief that should be corrected here. This is the wide-spread belief that the sari of today is of hoary antiquity. It is true that the word *sari* occurs in very ancient texts, but the word used there *meant a very different garment from that worn today*. One must beware of taking for granted that words of this type do not change their meanings. If you find literary evidence of the sari being worn in the time of the *Mahabharata*, you must not take it as evidence that the same garment was indicated as that which we now call by this name. It did not.

It is important to remember that the names of pieces of clothing to not change with the changes of shape. The English word 'coat' is a good example. The term occurs ever since English has been spoken, but the 'coat' of an Elizabethan courtier is not the same as the coat Charles Dickens wore; nor is my own coat much like the one that was sported by Mr Pickwick.

The word 'gown' too has changed its meaning, and so has 'frock'. 'Frock' was once widely used for a man's dress, now it is a woman's. And what, if you come to think of it, is a thing called 'a hat'? Cardinal Wolsey wore a thing called 'a hat', and so did King Edward VII: they were vastly different affairs, and neither bore much resemblance to an officer's 'hat' in the Royal Air Force, or to the plumed 'hat' of a Musketeer.

Littérateurs who find the word 'sari' in the poignant description in the *Mahabharata* of how Draupadi was put to shame, must not think that she wore a sari as we know it today, covering her hips thrown over one shoulder and allowed to fall back over the other. There is not the remotest doubt that Draupadi wore a small piece of cloth, called sari, wrapped round her waist only, and no upper garment; and when *that* sari was snatched from her hips, it was, indeed, a shameful act of male brutality. (Cp. Plates I, III, IV). That kind of sari could perhaps best be called a *dhoti* (as sometimes it is called in the India of today), or even a *sarong*, a Malay word, presumably borrowed from the Sanskrit and given the typical Malay ending—*ong*.

Dr Moti Chandra in his learned treatise uses the expression 'chhoti sari', *i.e. small* sari, whilst in other passages he calls the same garment a 'dhoti'. It amounts to the same thing. The difficulty is obvious, as this smaller garment, not sufficient to cover the upper body, was indeed called the sari in olden days.

Surprisingly enough, the present-day sari, which developed about the year A.D. 1780, did not develop from this older sari, but is the lengthening of that other garment, the *dupatta* or *orhni*, now tucked into the waistband, whilst the thing once called sari has turned, slowly, into a petticoat, worn under this much lengthened headkerchief, the *orhni*.

Whilst literary quotations must be handled with the utmost caution, because the meaning of a word changes with time, full reliance can be laid on the visual representations, such as the paintings and sculpture of the period. It is totally inconceivable that all the artists during two thousand years, all Indian painters and sculptors of the day painted and carved the things they saw, the kind of dress sported by the ladies and the gentlemen who were before their eyes.

Two strange exceptions are, to me, inexplicable, and need further investigation. One is the type of coatlike dress worn by the women shown in the Deogarh Dasavatara Temple relievos (U.P.), and by no one else in any other relievo carving at the end of the 6th century A.D. These appear to be Central Asian dresses of sorts, and though the Hun invasion belongs to this period, it is inexplicable why such costumes should have been depicted in this single monument and nowhere else.

The other is the occurrence in a few miniature paintings from round about the year 1570, made probably at Bijapur, of a long dress similar to the sari of today. These can be seen in Mr Basil Gray's *Treasures of Indian Miniatures*, Plates I and II. They certainly had no sequel, and remain isolated as a fashion.

Mention must be made here of the wall paintings in Tippu Sultan's hunting lodge at Seringapatam (Srirangapatnam) near Mysore. As the date of these paintings is known to within a few years—they can certainly be no later than 1799—it is of considerable interest that no sari is worn by any of the hundreds of women shown in these vast wall-paintings. Indeed, what they do wear is a kind of half-sari, somewhat like a stole, tucked into the waistband at one point, or allowed to hang freely in front, half covering the breasts and only partially the skirt-like petticoat that is worn underneath. It is the transitional stage that is known also from contemporary Rajasthani and Panjabi Hill paintings, when the headcovering becomes longer and is slowly draped further and further round the lower garment. It is also noteworthy that unmarried girls of South India often wear this brief sari (about 4 metres long) today and that it covers no more than a fourth of their petticoat or skirt. The conclusion is, therefore, justified that the modern, long sari developed about ten years earlier in Northern India.

INTRODUCTION

Theatrical and film producers dealing with the period preceding the 11th century A.D., when blouses were first worn in Gujarat at least, will have to find a way to approximate the dress of the earlier periods, without hurting modern propriety or being too anachronistic. Saris in the modern sense are out of the question, and anyone presenting Sakuntala or Sita or any other heroine of these old days with a sari, exposes himself to ridicule.

Two rather obvious solutions suggest themselves. One, and the less happy, is to use the upper garments shown in Ajanta and elsewhere as worn by maidservants and foreign female attendants. There is much to be said against this solution, this mixing of castes and classes, the only element that recommends it being that such a dress would at least not be anachronistic. It may not have been worn by the queen, but someone at her court in her day did wear such a costume.

Suggested solution for the theatre and the films: Cp. PLATE I. Flesh-coloured bodice with bead necklaces stitched on.

The other solution, suggested here is illustrated in the text-illustration on this page. This is to keep in all matters of detail to the contemporary dress worn by ladies, but to drape the breasts with a flesh-coloured bodice to which bead necklaces have been stitched. The figure here employed is the same fly-whisk bearer from the earliest extant Ajanta fresco who is shown, in her original appearance, in Plate I. It may be mentioned here that all the women, without exception, in that mural painting (150–100 B.C.) are depicted with uncovered breasts, both servants and queens.

Jewellery and personal ornament, to which only moderate attention has been paid in this booklet, deserve a special study. There have, indeed, been one or two serious studies on them, though their accurate dating needs much further checking. It is true that jewellery, by its very nature, does not change as easily as other fashions, for in India, as elsewhere, personal ornaments are inherited and worn by subsequent generations. Even today, young brides are given the jewellery of their mothers and grandmothers by way of dowry, and there is no reason to surmise that this was different in olden days, more addicted to the preservation of tradition than are these iconoclastic times.

With all that, it is easy to observe how fashions in jewellery also come and go, even if not so rapidly as do the fashions in those more destructible materials—textiles. For example, in Plates III and IV are shown enormous, outsize anklet rings not found, as far as I can see before the middle of the 2nd century A.D., and very rarely after the 3rd century, if at all. It is also observable that at one time anklets are worn singly and on one leg only—certainly in the 4th century this seems to have been the rule—at others both ankles bear rings.

Necklaces, earrings and diadems vary considerably over longer periods, and by the time the baroque period is in full swing, huge crowns are worn by many personages, as at Khajuraho, or in the cave sculptures of Aurangabad, where every dancing girl and musician sports a mighty crown, presumably stage jewellery of paste and tinsel. And yet there is no doubt at all that Indian jewellery was always as splendid and admirably wrought as it is today. Sculpture and painting show superbly designed chased metal (repoussé), elegantly set stones, ingeniously figured anklets, bracelets and armlets, and though bead and pearl necklaces abound, there were many other forms of neck ornaments, including pendants and moon-shaped breast-ornaments of chased gold and silver. Even if their fashions do not change as rapidly as those of dress, they deserve detailed study.

Local differences in fashion are much less marked than one might expect. One is surprised to find that dress in Andhra in the 1st to 4th century A.D., as shown in the sculptures of Amaravati, Nagarjunakonda and Jaggayyapeta, is almost identical with that worn further north at the same time, say in Mathura; but there are obvious local differences in Gandhara, a border area under western influence where Greco-Roman peplums were also worn, and variations grow when the North is overrun by Islamic invaders, around the 10th century A.D., whilst the South remains long unaffected. Not enough attention has been paid in this booklet to these small differences: they must be left to further investigators.

One marked difference between southern and northern costume is the way the dhoti or 'early sari' is worn. In Tamil land the dhoti is wound round the two legs separately and tightly, giving the appearance almost of tight trousers; when, at the same time, women in the North allow the cloth to hang loosely, almost skirt-like. The Chola queen in Plate XVII may be compared with the Orissan dancer in Plate XIV.

Soldiers and men-at-arms always constituted a separate class in dress. From the earliest times in sculptural and pictorial representation they appear wearing a coat or coat-of-mail (the chains are often clearly indicated), that bear a singular resemblance to Greek, or rather Roman, military wear. Whilst in other matters of dress, foreign influence (with the exception of Gandhara) is practically negligible, there seems to be good reason to conclude that here direct borrowing has been at work. It is known for certain that Chandragupta the Maurya emperor learned his military organization from Seleucus before he conquered half of India; and his successor, Asoka the Great, kept close contact with his western neighbours in Iran, then completely Hellenised. His inscriptions mention the contemporary kings of the Hellenic East to whom he had sent messengers or ambassadors (*duta*). It is also interesting to note that in the earliest extant paintings at Ajanta the officers and other ranks wear identical coats and the only difference between officers and men is that the latter wear no turbans (Plate II, *a*; note that the king in the same Plate wears sandals, probably another borrowing from the West of Asia).

Kings, like other men, wear no upper garment unless they are going into battle. In Northern India a kind of blanket or wrap, somewhat like a modern *chadar*, is sometimes worn loosely over the shoulder, and allowed to fall one way or the other. They may well have been used in the cold weather, but I know of no sculptural or pictorial example showing such a wrap being draped round the body. In South India, where tradition is more strictly followed, the king must go to the temple even today with his breast bare.

It will be observed that in the first half of this book there is a certain preponderance of feminine fashions over the male, whilst when we come to the Mughals, the Plates show more masculine dresses than feminine—however much I tried to balance the illustrations to equalize the difference.

But this is the natural result of two different attitudes. It does not need much acumen to observe that Buddhist and Hindu monuments take far more interest in women than in men. Ajanta is full of graceful women, and the number of male personages is far smaller than that of women. On the other hand, the world of the Islamic invaders and of the luxurious courts of Delhi and Agra was a world of men, for men, a world of warriors, princes, hunters, courtiers, with their women folk relegated behind veils and sheltered behind latticed windows. Indeed, you can look through many an album (*muraqqa*) of Mughal miniature paintings and find hardly a counterfeit of a woman in it.

In Rajasthani and Hill paintings women again preponderate, or at least equal the men in numbers; and there would be anything up to a dozen cowherd girls in some paintings to one Krishna dallying with them.

This book does not deal with the prehistoric Harappan civilization, as the materials unearthed so far at Harappa, Mohenjo-daro and related sites are not sufficient to form the basis of serious study. A priest in a robe, a totally naked dancing girl, some seals showing dancing girls at a sacrifice dressed in what looks like skirts, is about all the evidence we possess so far.

Whilst this book attempts to exclude all that is worn only by foreign servants and entertainers, whether at Taxila, at Ajanta, at Nagarjunakonda or in Sanchi, foreign influences become so important from the 13th century onwards that a distinction becomes impossible. I refer not only to the fact that Islamic dress has changed Indian male fashions completely, so that even the cowherd god Krishna is shewn in numerous miniatures dressed in a Mughal *jama* (coat) with a dashing *patka* (sash), but to the equally important fact that with the arrival of the Muslims the attire of women in India underwent a fundamental change. This revolutionary change was much slower in the South, no doubt, than in the North, but the change was basic everywhere.

It is difficult to escape the conclusion, even if the evidence is not absolutely conclusive, that the wide adoption of the typical Indian 'three-piece dress' of women was the result, direct or indirect, of the invasions from the West and North-west. This typical three-piece dress of the Indian woman is the bodice (*choli*), the skirt (*ghaghra*) and the head-kerchief (*orhni*); the first two are sewn and tailored garments, unknown in pre-Islamic times, when only military coats were sewn.

It is, however, necessary to emphasize the fact that only the idea of these novel garments was borrowed from the invaders, not the shape. There is no evidence whatever that identical skirts and bodices had ever been worn by, say, the women of Persia or of Central Asia. Indeed, Mughal princesses, women at the court and in the Muslim harem wore very different dresses based on Iranian models, some of which are illustrated in Plates XXI and XXVIII, *c*.

It is not without interest to mention that the men in India were more inclined in these periods (as they are in modern times) to accept foreign modes than their women. Whilst the mass of women in India has never accepted Iranian costume (except here and there in the Panjab, and the hills), the impact of the Mughal court dress on rajas and men of class was decisive. Miniature paintings of the Rajputs both in the plains and in the hills show thousands of men dressed *á la* Mughal, while hardly any women are depicted as wearing any other attire but the three-piece dress evolved by India. It was the men again who had accepted much of the western way of dressing when the British came, and in these days coats and trousers are worn by millions of Indians.

The sacred thread, the *yajnopavita*, contrary to present-day custom, was in olden days worn both by men *and women*. There are numerous sculptures and paintings showing women wearing the sacred thread and already in the early period of Amaravati, a Buddhist monument, women are seen with the *yajnopavita*. One such example is shown in Plate XI, in which the woman has the sacred thread, and the man is without it.

A word must be said here about the ancient stage. Those who attempt a reconstruction of the Sanskrit stage, as it was in its heyday, will have their hands full of problems. There is irrefutable evidence that the ancient Indian stage was highly stylized, artificial, full of conventions and symbolism. In many ways the nearest comparison is the present-day Kathakali dance drama of Malabar. We have it on the evidence of the treatise entitled *Bharata-Natya-Sastra*, the greatest extant authority on dramatics, that actors and actresses painted their skins in colours considered suitable to their roles. As in Kathakali, the hero would be painted bright red or green or pink, others would appear as dark brown or black and their costumes were much farther removed from 'realism' than those in Shakespeare's days, when Julius Caesar or Timon of Athens or Romeo came on the stage dressed in Elizabethan fashions. It seems that the Indian actor was dressed in clothes that were not worn even by his contemporaries. I have made some reference to these matters in my article 'Five Thousand Years of Indian Theatre'. (*Western Railway Annual*, 1955-56, pp. 63-67.)

To re-establish these conventions, now almost totally forgotten, is a task wrought with endless difficulties. It is much easier to attempt to present on the stage men and women as they actually appeared in life in, say, the times of Kalidasa's

Sakuntala or Sudraka's *The Little Clay Cart*. There is no need to commit anachronisms. Ample material is available about the type of dress worn by all classes, the only practical difficulty being the one already referred to; the undraped breasts of women. And although a very great deal of work is necessary to make an exhaustive and reliable history of Indian dress, the examples given in this booklet should be of some help to producers.

II. MATERIALS

Only the scantiest knowledge exists about the materials of which dress was made in ancient times. That cotton was widely used is obvious; for cotton, as far as we know, is altogether an Indian invention (as silk is Chinese), and it occurs, without any doubt, at about 2300 B.C. at the prehistoric site of Mohenjo-daro in Sindh. There is evidence that it was exported from the Indus Valley in prehistoric times, and there is a good deal of probability that it was the *kaunakes* of the old Greeks, known to Mesopotamia long before the Ionians reached the shores of the Aegean.

On the other hand, our information as to when silk was first introduced into India is extremely sketchy. Dr Moti Chandra, in his learned Hindi book already quoted, takes great pains to discover when silk was first known to Indians, and some of his literary researches into this question are of considerable value. What is certain is that that great scholar, Panini, mentions what must be taken to be silk; but as the date of Panini is as uncertain as most things in those remote days of Sanskrit literature, all one can say is that silk may have been known, indeed probably was known, as an imported article around the 2nd century B.C., or possibly in the 3rd. It would be rash to surmise that the Emperor Asoka possessed more than a few pieces of it, and I believe it to be quite unrealistic to think that ladies and gentlemen could afford to buy in great quantities a material that was brought laboriously by caravans travelling across the Takla Makan Desert of Central Asia and over dangerous mountain passes above 16,000 feet high.

It is far more likely that silk from China reached India in good quantities when it also reached the Roman Empire at the height of its luxury, that is to say, in the 1st to the 4th centuries A.D., when the Great Silk Route of Serindia, so brilliantly described by Sir Aurel Stein, passed through Indian territory, *via* the Kabul Valley. For the Kabul Valley was then part of the Kingdom of Gandhara, an Indian Buddhist country, ruled by a Central Asian Dynasty, the Kushanas, who kept in close contact with their home country on the borders of China.

It would be interesting to know, too, when silk was first *produced* in India. Dr Moti Chandra discusses this problem with great acumen and learning, and comes to some valuable conclusions. One of the difficulties that confronts the scholar is the fact that materials, such as *simul* silk (*Bombax malabaricum*), that closely resemble cocoon silk, were produced in India, and are still being produced in these days.

In the description of Plate IX in this book reference is made to silk. To all appearances the painters of Ajanta were acquainted with it in the 6th and 7th centuries A.D. and, in fact, it is highly probable that by that time silk was more commonly used by princes and the rich. For all the previous centuries, nevertheless, we must postulate cotton as the common material for dress.

It is a strange discovery to make from extant painting in a country as fond of colour as is the India of today that a most moderate use was made of dyed material or colour in dress until the 12th century. From then onwards much bolder dyeing and printing of cloth is evidenced in the Gujarati miniature paintings. In the 6th and 7th century mural paintings in Ajanta a few examples of striking textile patterns are shown (although never in strident colours), but before that, and indeed long after those few examples, the majority of textiles worn are either plain white, or relieved only with a few stripes, or ribbons of check patterns; and those, too, in a few colours only. Red and black stripes on a white ground predominate; even the famous guardians (*dvarapalas*), whose painted dress survives almost intact in two of the Ajanta caves, wear the simplest of loin garments (*dhotis*) with stripes in those two colours. There is plenty of evidence that the elaborately ornate textiles are worn exclusively by foreigners, *e.g.*, attendant girls holding umbrellas or other royal paraphernalia.

In the 12th to 15th centuries, richly decorated and patterned cloth, mostly print is amply evidenced by Gujarati miniatures and the early Rajasthani (Malwa, *etc.*) miniature paintings. Some examples are reproduced in Plates XVI and XVII.

With the establishment of the Mughal court, aristocratic, luxury-loving and wealthy, follows an age of bright colours, rich designs and tremendous variety, especially in brocades. Only a little can be shown of this court fashion in an elementary book of this nature, but there are hundreds of miniatures to study, and not the least striking development among the non-Mughal people of this period—the Rajputs of the plains and the Panjab hills—is the love for large, bright patches of brilliant colour (not evidenced anywhere in the earlier centuries, say in Buddhist art), such as fiery crimsons, burning vermilions, stark blues, blazing yellows and glorious greens. In this respect, the Hindus outdid the Mughals.

Well into the 16th and 17th centuries, stripes continue to be *the* favourite pattern for Hindu and Muslim women alike, especially for the skirts (*ghaghras*). Mughal court dress demands patterned brocades, embroidery and velvets; whilst most of the lovely ladies of Rajasthan and Kangra would wear unpatterned, plain bright three-piece dresses (the *ghaghra* often striped), with the head-kerchief (*orhni*), becoming more and more important as a strikingly brilliant patch of bright colour; although sometimes it is a transparent white veil with small patterns, as in plates XXIV and XXVIII.

I do not know when velvet was first used in India. Someone ought to study the problem, as well as that of linen. Velvet was known to imperial Rome, and may have been known to contemporary Gandhara. But there is no evidence known to me before the age of the Muslim rulers. The rulers of the Deccanese kingdoms, including Adil Shah II, used velvet.

As to linen, it stands to reason to presume that it was produced in Northern India, where flax grew abundantly. Here, too, however, convincing evidence is lacking.

With so much ignorance about materials it is safe to assume that cotton was—as it certainly is today—the most widely worn textile, from prehistoric times onwards. That the thinnest cotton-muslin was made of it, is amply proved by monuments, especially painting. It would be difficult, indeed, to explain in any other way the diaphanous dress in which men and women appear in hundreds of sculptures and paintings. Judging from present-day facts, the ordinary handloom weaver was capable of weaving extremely fine and thin cotton stuff; some of it, worn now-a-days in remote villages, is a marvel of skill and refined dexterity.

As an interesting postscript to this chapter on materials, I would remind the reader that when, in the 16th and early 17th century, Western tradesmen, English, Dutch, Spanish, Portuguese and French, started commerce with India, their chief import from India, apart from spices, was *calico*, the cotton cloth from Calicut on the Malabar coast. Not silk, by any means, although the nobles and the rich of India must by that time have worn a good deal of silk in and around the opulent courts of the princes. Silks, brocades and velvets were very well known in Renaissance Europe and Elizabethan England, but they came from the Levant trade.

It was in about 1670 that Dacca muslins were first brought to England. The word 'muslin' comes from the name of the Mesopotamian city, Mosul, from which the Levantine trade first obtained delicately woven cotton stuffs.

III. MILESTONES

The history of Indian dress, promised in the title of this book, is found in the plates. It is first and foremost a visual history, and the commentary given opposite each plate only assists in the more accurate fixing of an image.

Nevertheless, it seems worth while to mark in a few brief pages the milestones of this history. They are few, because certain basic fashions, changing slowly in minor detail, remained almost stationary for long periods. These notes are brief, for the unfolding of this history is given much more lucidly in the plates.

From the earliest recorded time—recorded, that is, in visual monuments and not in literary remains discounted to a great extent in this book—that of the Emperor Asoka, both the men and women of India wore one piece of garment: a plain length of cloth, sometimes ornamented with coloured stripes, which they wound round their waist and tucked into a waistband (presumably a cotton string, as today). Sometimes the end in front was gathered between the legs and pulled to the back, where the end was again tucked into the same waistband.

In these early periods sewn garments were not worn by women at all, and only very rarely by men—mainly the military—and we meet the first stitched pieces in about the 11th century. The army wore tailored and sewn coats from the 3rd century B.C., but women had no sewn skirts before the 13th century.

Neither men nor women in ordinary walks of life, except the military and foreign court employees and visiting dancing teams, wore an upper garment to cover their breasts.

However, a scarf or shawl is frequently found, in a variety of thickness and length. This is thrown across the back of the neck, casually passed over the arm, and sometimes used as a head covering, rather as the Panjabi woman wears her *dupatta* in these days. There is no evidence anywhere that this headkerchief or scarf was used in antiquity in order to hide the breasts. Even in the 12th century, when bodices or blouses are worn for the first time, this scarf has no such purpose; not in antiquity. It is much more likely that in Northern India, where the winter is and was harsh, men and women wore a thicker material for a kind of shawl, and wrapped themselves up in it when the weather demanded.

There is, however, not one sculpture or painting known to me that shows any one in this dress draped in a warm wrap before the 16th century A.D.

For a wrap, see Plates V and VI; for 12th century scarves, see Plate XVI.

The military dress ('uniform' would be an anachronistic term), from the first extant representations (Bharhut, Sanchi, Ajanta Cave X, roughly 2nd and 1st centuries B.C.) bears a marked resemblance to Western Asian, hence Greco-Roman and Alexandrian, military wear. Just as today, the uniforms in all the armies of the world show much similarity, so the mail coat, the belt for carrying side arms (sword, dagger, dirk), and even the protection of arms and legs, was much the same in the ancient world, from Rome to the Far East. The Greeks learned a great deal from the Persians, the Romans from the Greeks, and all three of them from the Egyptians. Thus the men-at-arms and the soldiers in the first few hundred years of documented history in India look rather like their Western Asian counterparts: they wear the same kind of coats and belts; though officers in India wore turbans, whilst 'other ranks' went about bareheaded. Boots, however, were hardly ever worn by the Indian army.

It has already been noted in the General Introduction that the name of the bodice, *choli*, seems to come from the word *chola*, body. More interesting is the etymology of the name of another feminine garment, the *pasvaj*. (The spelling *pesh-waz* seems to be erroneous). This is of Iranian origin and was used in the Mughal court, and it survives, often as a ceremonial dress, but still worn by older women-folk of all classes, in some of the Panjab hill tracts. It is a chemise or 'princess' gown-like frock, reaching from the neck down to the ankles, with long sleeves, and often with a narrow waist. Now the word *pasvaj* appears to come from the verb *pasujna*, 'to stitch, to sew with running stitches', so that the word registers and retains, as it were, the surprise of the Indian feminine world when it first met a stitched garment—not just a plain piece of cloth wrapped round the body to which the women of India had been accustomed.

It is unnecessary, and would be tautological, to tell of the small changes in the *dhoti*, the lower garment—the only one—from the 2nd century B.C. to the 12th century A.D.; how it bacame now longer, now shorter, and how its ends were gathered now this way, now that; for all this is clearly told in the succession of pictures that follows, and in the descriptive matter opposite each page.

But it is worth noting that the metal, and sometimes bejewelled, belt (in Sanskrit *mekhala*, though other names also occur), worn at least from Asoka's days, seems to have disappeared for a few centuries (Plates V, VI, VII, VIII and IX), or was at least rarely worn, only to return again, with great éclat, in the 8th century. From then onwards there is a bold development, on baroque and later rococo lines, when this belt becomes the chief ornament of apparel, as it were, with hanging loops and pearls, beads and precious stones, just as all personal ornament in this late period turns to ornate riches and voluptuous elaboration. And though men did not wear the *mekhala* (girdle), at one time at least, urged by a penchant for baroque over-decoration, they too wore a bejewelled waistbelt, though higher up, a few inches above the girdle. This was the period when men went about in fanciful and most effeminate-looking hair styles, with coifs and buns of affected shapes. (Plates X and XI).

The impact of the Islamic invasions on Indian attire was extensive.

There is a true milestone with the arrival of Iranian and Central Asian fashions. Not only do women now accept sewn garments, which they had never worn before, and not only do they henceforth cover their upper bodies, which they never did before, but the dress of the men is totally changed.

During the reign of the Timurid dynasty, the upper class, men all over Northern India and the Deccan, from palace servants and Rajput warriors to well-to-do merchants and princes, gradually adopted some variation of the *jama*, the buttoned coat of the Mughals. Buttoned coats of any description were formerly unknown in India. The women of India, much more conservative than their men-folk, wore the three-piece costume still typical of most of Rajasthan: the skirt (*ghaghra*), the bodice (*choli*) and the head-kerchief (*orhni* or *dupatta*), But the men dressed themselves in imitation of court wear, and we see in the contemporary miniature the heroes of the *Ramayana* and the *Mahabharata*, as well as the lover in the delectable *Nayika-Nayaka* series (love affairs in pictures), dressed in elegant Mughal court turbans, and the latest fashions in buttoned coats. (Cp. Plates XXII, XXIV, XXVIII). Yet there is nothing more un-Mughal than these Hindu epics, or the loves of Krishna the cowherd-god.

The women of India have hardly ever adopted purely foreign fashions. An exception is the Panjabi *shalvar* (trousers) and *kamiz* (shirt), and the *pasvaj* already mentioned, which are frequently seen in the love scenes of the Nayika series. During the Hellenistic period (1st century B.C. to 5th century A.D.) in Gandhara a few women wore Greco-Roman peplum-like dresses, but the majority went about in the same apparel as their sisters elsewhere in India. The present-day adoption by fashionable women of frocks and jeans and trousers is something for which there is no parallel in the past history of the country.

The constant fashion changes at the Mughal imperial courts of Agra, Delhi, and Lahore (the emperors resided alternately in these three forts, and often went camping) need, in fact, a much more detailed study than this booklet can provide. Among the works of several scholars who have studied this period, that of Dr Hermann Goetz on Mughal court attire is the most important.

The stern, military simplicity and 'functionalism' of the Emperors Babar (Plate XIX) and Humayun, founders of the

Timurid dynasty's reign in India, gradually give way to more fanciful, splendid, aristocratic attire, in richer materials, as the Mughals settle down to enjoy the fruits of their phenomenal conquests, and as they become much more part of India. In this love of brilliant colours and expensive materials, as well as of profuse personal ornament, they have learnt a great deal from the Hindu rajas. It must be remembered that Akbar's successor, Jehangir, was born of one of Akbar's Hindu wives, a Rajput princess.

The characteristic dress in Akbar's earlier years was made of solid, opaque material, a *jama* that had a skirt with four, later with six, hanging points. (Cp. Plates XX and XXI). But towards the end of his reign, this upper garment, worn over *tång pai-jamas* (tight trousers, from which the 'jodhpurs' of today descend), became diaphanous: a typical Hindu influence, natural in a hot climate, and based on the age-old love for thin material in India. And this transparent material, later without the hanging points, went out of fashion soon after Jehangir ascended the throne. (Cp. Plate XXIII).

Jehangir's rich silk and brocade *jamas* were worn with a boldly developed sash, the *kamarband* (the English 'cummerbund') or rather the *patka*. This varied almost from year to year, with embroidered or woven patterns, often of delicately designed flowers, sometimes with geometric patterns. Even women adopted it, enlarging it, especially in Rajasthan and the Southern courts of various Deccani rulers, into what looks at times almost an apron. This kind of *patka* starts as a narrow band on the stomach and broadens out near the foot into a great expanse of decorated cloth, an inverted V shape (Plate XXIV *a* and *b*).

But this apron-like *patka*, or sash of the Deccan and the Rajasthani and other Hindu women, was worn by them over a *ghaghra* or skirt (not a *jama* coat); and at the same time, around 1750, the *orhni*, the head-kerchief, started growing longer and more important. This story leads on to the invention of the sari in the sense in which it is used today; a word (it must be repeated) that has a basically different meaning from the former connotation of the 'sari' in ancient literature, where it was used to mean the lower garment, the *dhoti* of today. The modern sari is the *dupatta* or *orhni* grown long and tucked around the skirt, whilst the old skirt has now become invisible, a petticoat *under* the sari. For details cp. Plates XXVIII and XXIX, the last plate showing the actual birth of the modern sari. It is not without historical and psychological interest to point out that *the sari has now, during the last ten years or so, undergone a further change, as it is no more used by the middle and upper classes to cover the head.*

In South India, where for hundreds of years the fashions had been identical or almost identical with those north of the Vindhya Mountains, the impact of Muslim fashions was, naturally, much less felt. The Mughals have never effectively conquered the South, except the Deccan, and bare-breasted women go about up to the present day in Kerala and Andhra as they did two thousand three hundred years ago. The exact date when the sari was adopted by South Indians is not known to me. And though itinerant English painters show women wearing saris in the *middle* of the 19th century in the South, to this author it appears that in many parts of South India the sari is hardly older than this century. Elderly Tamil ladies assure me that their mothers did not wear *full* saris that covered the whole of the skirt, and many wore only a blouse and skirt, as young girls do in the Tamil country today.

With the beginning of the 19th century, in any case, the western conquests, especially those of the East India Company and of the Portuguese, bring a confusion that demands another book. By the end of the 19th century the influence of western dress on the *men* of India is tremendous, and so it remains to this day. Not only townsfolk, but peasants too wear coats and shirts and trousers aptly or clumsily modelled on the British-Western style; not to speak of Hawaian bush-shirts, tweed suits and dinner jackets. Shorts, an innovation by British planters and army personnel, can now be seen in the remote hamlets of India.

That the women remain hardly touched by these fashions is still noticeable; although in the last few years one has frequently seen fashionable women of the upper classes sporting drain-pipe trousers, jeans, shorts and bikinis, and in elegant women's colleges you now meet girls belonging to any community, Hindu, Muslim, Christian, Parsi, or Sikh, wearing western blouses and skirts. History, perhaps, is not repeating itself this time. But some one else has to write the history of the nylon age.

LIST OF PLATES

Plate I : 150-100 B.C. Lady-in-waiting on a king. *a :* detail of metal belt. *b :* detail of a turban with striped material worn by woman. *c :* form of head covering. *d :* back of head covered with turban and plaits of hair. *e :* another type of necklace.

Plate II : 150-100 B.C. A king at home. *a :* a palace officer, or officer-at-arms. *b :* detail of turban and earring.

Plate III : 100-150 A.D. Woman carrying food in basket and a pitcher. *a :* detail of belt clasp. *b :* different style of necklace of long beads. *c :* men's turbans, front and side view, with 'turret' top. *d :* differently decorated anklets.

Plate IV : 150-200 A.D. Man and woman from South India; woman in slight undress (without sacred thread).

Plate V : 200-300 A.D. Man of noble class. *a :* solid breast ornament with precious stones. *b :* armlet with stones, and manner of tying. *c :* different style turban with crest. *d :* sandal with inlaid stones.

Plate VI : 200-300 A.D. Lady of noble class. *a :* example of ribbon as hair ornament. *b :* detail of metal belt with chased medallions. *c :* back view of head of woman, with 'Sasanian' ribbons and plait of hair.

Plate VII : 400-410 A.D. Lady on way to shrine. *a :* examples of other cloth patterns of the period. *b :* Side and back view of manner of tying the *dhoti*.

Plate VIII : 550-600 A.D. Girl attending on princess, holding a fan. *a :* cap of medical nurse. *b :* groom dressed in striped *tahmad.*

Plate IX : 650-700 A.D. Princess walking in the street. *a :* queen seated in palace pavilion. *b :* examples of 'halo' style of head-dress from the end of the century.

Plate X : 650-700 A.D. Gentleman of the princely class. *a :* male head, with handle-bar moustache and long hair. *b :* King Mahendravarman of South India.

Plate XI : About 740 A.D. A military gentleman and his lady, the latter wearing a 'halo' head-dress.

Plate XII : About 850-900 A.D. A Bengali lady. *a :* similar head-dress, but with jewels, from Bihar. *b :* two examples of belt chains. *c :* example of an armlet. *d :* necklace of different shape from Orissa. *e :* a head-dress from Gwalior, Rajasthan, with jewellery.

Plate XIII : 961-973 A.D. Male musician playing the barrel drum. *a :* and *b :* Male beard and male hair-dress. *c :* back view of another drummer. *Right bottom :* dancing girl.

Plate XIV : About 1000 A.D. Dancing girl from Orissa *a :* design on textile from Orissa. *b :* two kinds of bracelets.

Plate XV : About 1100 A.D. Portrait of a queen from South India, also showing back.

Plate XVI : About 1127 A.D. Gujarati lady of court. *a :* male hair wear and beard. *b :* examples of scarf patterns. *c :* examples (four) of textile designs.

Plate XVII : 13th century A.D. Portrait of a Chola queen. *a :* enlarged design of pattern on the queen's *dhoti.*

LIST OF PLATES

Plate XVIII : *14th century* A.D. Warrior chief of Andhra, fully accoutred, cutting his own throat.

Plate XIX : *Babar's time (1526-1530).* The Emperor Babar. *a* : examples of turbans worn by retainer and a companion of the Emperor. *b* : royal retainer with halbred. *c* : examples of shoes as worn by the Emperor and others when not in riding boots.

Plate XX : *Akbar's Court (1556-1605).* Portrait of a nobleman in violet coat, holding a sword.

Plate XXI : *Akbar's time (1556-1605).* Maidservant of the palace offering wine. *a* : turban and head of an old man of the street. *b* : an old woman of the people wrapped in a big shawl. *Bottom right* : uniformed palace servant in waiting on the Emperor.

Plate XXII : *Rajasthan, 1570.* Man of military class, with dagger. *a* : Rajasthani woman seated. *b* : village woman of Rajasthan at the well *c* : textile patterns of the time, and, *on right*, embroidered sleeve of bodice.

Plate XXIII : *Jehangir (1605-1627), c. 1609.* The Emperor with orange-red turban and a cream-coloured coat.

Plate XXIV : *Deccan, 1625.* Hindu woman tossing a swing for Hindola Raga. *c* : Hindu gentleman. *d* : samples of sash patterns and of tassels and pompoms.

Plate XXV : *Jehangir, c. 1620. Top* : The Prince Khusrau in a white coat, seated in front of a bolster. *Bottom* : A falconer (Khan Alam) in a short coat, with a row of buttons and a sash. *a* : and *b* : two examples of designs on ends of sashes, *a* : woven cypresses, *b* : embroidered tulips.

Plate XXVI : *Shahjehan (1627-1659) in 1640.* The Emperor in a feathered turban of gold cloth, a long coat with lapel flaps, a waistband and sash, striped trousers, and holding a cavalry sword.

Plate XXVII : Aurangzeb (1659-1707), about 1665. The Emperor seated, holding a flywhisk (not shewn here), wearing a dark green coat with plant pattern scattered over it, a gold sash, a jade-handled dagger, from which hangs a pendant ending in rows of pearls. *Below* : examples of turbans with feather ornaments.

Plate XXVIII : North India, 1780. *a* : shows the male attire of Hindu aristocracy, on the model of court wear; the other designs show the three types of feminine wear in vogue : *top*, three-piece dress of bodice, skirt and diaphanous head-kerchief. *b* : the head-kerchief of more solid material, much longer than before, and tucked into the waistband in front : first step towards the sari : *c* : the *pasvaj*, a long, frock-like garment of Iranian origin.

Plate XXIX : Kangra, 1790. The complete sari, now tucked in all round, or almost all round the waistband, practically covering the skirt, and partially covering the breasts.

Plate XXX : Delhi, circa 1820. Gentleman at the Court of Delhi, wearing a heavy coat with gold braid round borders and side slit; a plastron-like piece is visible under the neck. The turban is rather flat. The other turban examples show a variety of wear fashionable at the beginning of the 19th century. The bottom figure is a pedlar from a Patna painting, in a white coat with plastron, and a flat turban.

ABBREVIATIONS IN REFERENCES FOR PLATES

The references made in this section are mainly to books widely obtainable and of recent date. The abbreviations mostly used are:

AIP : K.B. De Codrington, John Irwin and Basil Gray. *The Art of Indian and Pakistan*, edited by Sir Basil Ashton. London, 1950.

JRAS : *Journal of the Royal Asiatic Society*, London.

Kramrisch : Stella Kramrisch. *The Art of India*. Phaidon Press, London, 1954.

Kramrisch, *Deccan* : Stella Kramrisch. *A Survey of Painting in the Deccan*. London, 1954.

Marg : *Marg*, a magazine of architecture and art, edited by Dr Mulk Anand. Bombay, 1947 onwards.

Rowland : Benjamin Rowland. *The Art and Architecture of India*. In the Pelican History of Art. Penguin Books, London, 1954.

Yazdani : Ghulam Yazdani and others. *Ajanta*. Four volumes of text and four volumes of plates. Reference always to the plate volumes. Oxford University Press, London, 1931-1955.

Zimmer : Heinrich Zimmer. *The Art of Indian Asia*. Completed by Joseph Campbell. Bollingen Series, New York, 1955. Two volumes; reference always to the volume of plates.

A more detailed Bibliography will be found at the end of this book.

PLATE I

There is good evidence for the dress of the period 150-100 B.C., the most ample being the earliest relievo carvings at Bharhut and the earliest paintings in the Ajanta caves. Avoiding all the examples showing gods and godlings (yakshas, yakshinis, vrikshakas and other supernatural beings), all the examples shewn in Plates I and II are ordinary mortals. The main figure in this plate is a king's maidservant or lady-in-waiting. The turban in (*b*) is worn by a dancing girl. The turban and plaits of hair in (*d*) belong to one of the ladies-in-waiting in Prince Gautama's royal palace.

In this age, and for hundreds of years after this, all such women wear a single piece of cloth, a *dhoti* or sarong-like cloth draped round the waist and held up by a metal girdle (*mekhala*). It is made of such thin material that the legs and privy parts are fairly visible through it. A thin ribbon-like waistband falls over the girdle and in front, between the legs. A scarf or kerchief (*dupatta, orhni*) is sometimes worn. Women wear a turban just as frequently as men do, which is not too often. The *dupatta* is a head covering and is never long enough to cover the breasts. Jewellery is sparse and of great simplicity. The head-dress in the case of women is either plaits or a bun. Little is known of coloured materials, but from the Ajanta murals it appears that white, with some little red pattern (stripes perhaps) was mainly worn. Many women wear no anklets.

REFERENCES

Yazdani, *Ajanta*, vol. III. pl. XXX, (*c*) and others. Also pl. XXVI. Kramrisch, *Deccan*, pl. I Bharhut : any publication, everywhere. Fabri, for plaits and head-dress, *JRAS.*, London, July 1931. For Ajanta, Cave X, also *Marg*-IX, 1. (December 1955, two folding plates). Rowland, pl. 17. Kramrisch. pl. 16. Zimmer, pl. 32 (*a*), 36 (*b*).

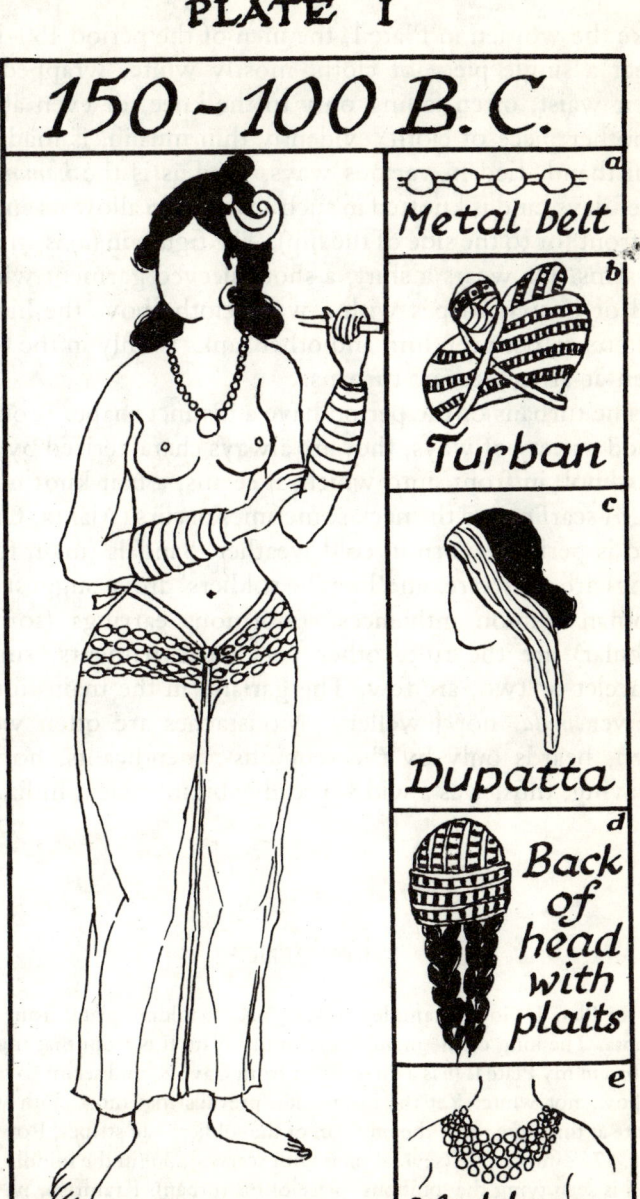

PLATE II

Like the women in Plate I, the men of the period 150-100 B.C. wear a single piece of cloth, mostly white, wrapped round their waist, often falling only to the knee, or even above it. Another piece of cloth, evidently thin muslin, is made into a waistband, tied in various ways, used as is the *kamarband* of later days, and is knotted in such a way as to allow its end to fall in front (or to the side of the hip). The figure in (*a*) is an officer-at-arms. He wears a shirt, a short-sleeved garment with dark red or brown stripes with a waist-cloth above the hips. The difference between him and other ranks is only in the turban : men-at-arms wear no turbans.

The turbans of the period have a distinct shape. Wound in a good variety of ways, they are always characterized by a bulbous knob in front, into which, it seems, a hair knot is woven (?). A scarf round the neck sometimes occurs (Ajanta, Cave X), and is perhaps worn in cold weather. Sandals (main figure, a king) are very rare, and like the soldiers' dress, suggest Greco-Roman fashion influences. Enormous earrings (sometimes tubular) are the rule, other personal ornaments, such as a bracelet or two, are few. The garland in the main figure is a flower *mala*, not jewellery. Moustaches are often worn by men, beards only by the religious : mendicants, holy men. Shaving, thus, was a wide-spread habit in ancient India.

REFERENCES

As for Plate I. Good examples in *Marg*, IX, 1, folding plate, from Cave X, Ajanta. The king of the main figure in my Plate II is from that mural. The turban in my Plate II (*b* is a direct copy from Cave X, and seems to be Naples Yellow, not white. Yet the impression prevails that most cloth was plain white at this time, only the uniform of the soldiers had stripes, Rowland, pl. 15 *a*, 17. Zimmer, 32 (several men with scarves), 36 (in the middle picture a man is seen tying the 'bulbous' piece of his turban). Kramrisch, pl. 16 (men with 'bulb', women's turbans without it), pl. 18 (king and attendants).

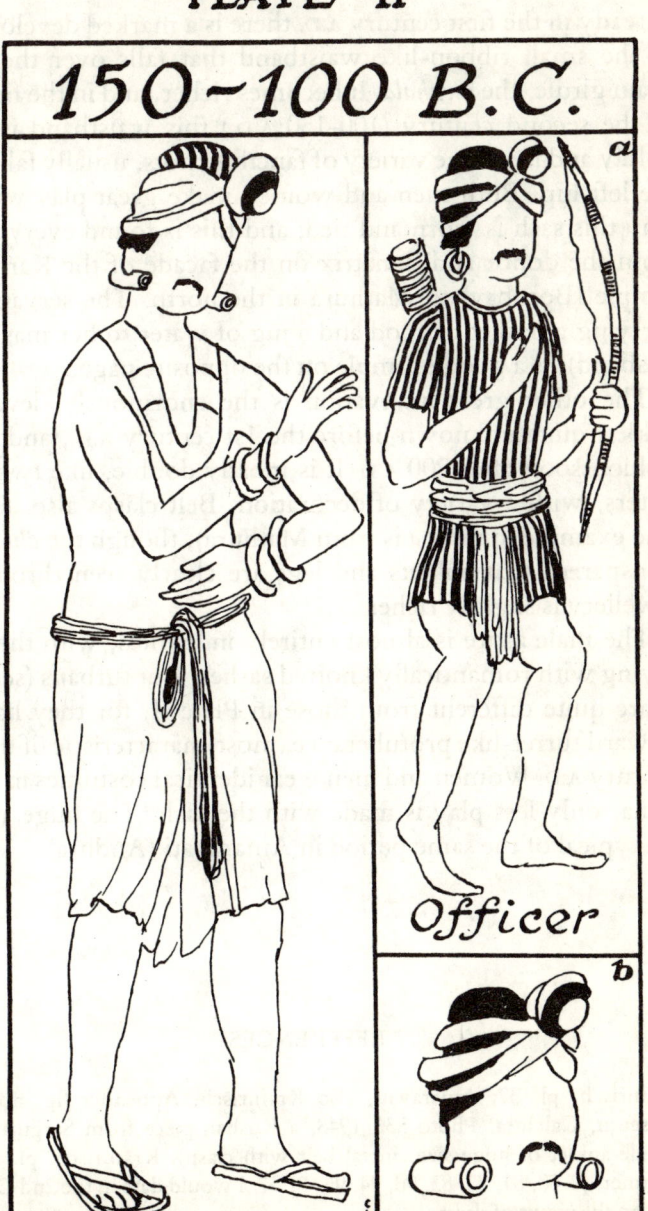

PLATE III

Already in the first century A.D. there is a marked development of the small ribbon-like waistband that falls over the metal chain girdle, the *mekhala*. It becomes richer, and in the first half of the second century (100-150 A.D.) this waistband is worn boldly and in a large variety of fanciful knots, usually falling on the left hip. Both men and women make great play with the way this sash is worn and tied; and this is found everywhere, from the donor and donatrix on the facade of the Karle cave temple (Bombay) to Mathura in the north. The servant girl, carrying a basket of food and a jug of water to her master (or husband), is a good example on the opposite page.

The other great innovation is the enormously developed anklet, quite unknown before the 1st century A.D., and out of fashion soon after 200 A.D. It is mostly double, like two huge fetters, with a variety of decoration. Belt clasps also develop (the example in inset *a* is from Mathura), though the *dhoti* is so transparent that anklets and legs are clearly seen through it. Jewellery is slightly richer.

The male attire is almost entirely indentical, with the same toying with romantically knotted sashes. But turbans (see inset *c*) are quite different from those in Plate II, for they have an upward turret-like protuberance, most characteristic of the 2nd century A.D. Women and men wear identical costumes in South India, only less play is made with the sash. The huge anklets are typical of the same period in Amaravati (Andhra).

REFERENCES

Kramrisch, pl. 37; Amaravati, also Kramrisch, Appendix fig. 8. Indian Museum, Calcutta, Photo 536/1948, a Kushan piece from Sarguja, M.P. (single anklet of huge size, metal belt with clasp). Kramrisch, pl. 26, 27, Zimmer, pl. 80, 81, 82, 83, 90, 94, 95. Pl. 37 I would date in the 2nd Century A.D. on the count of dress.

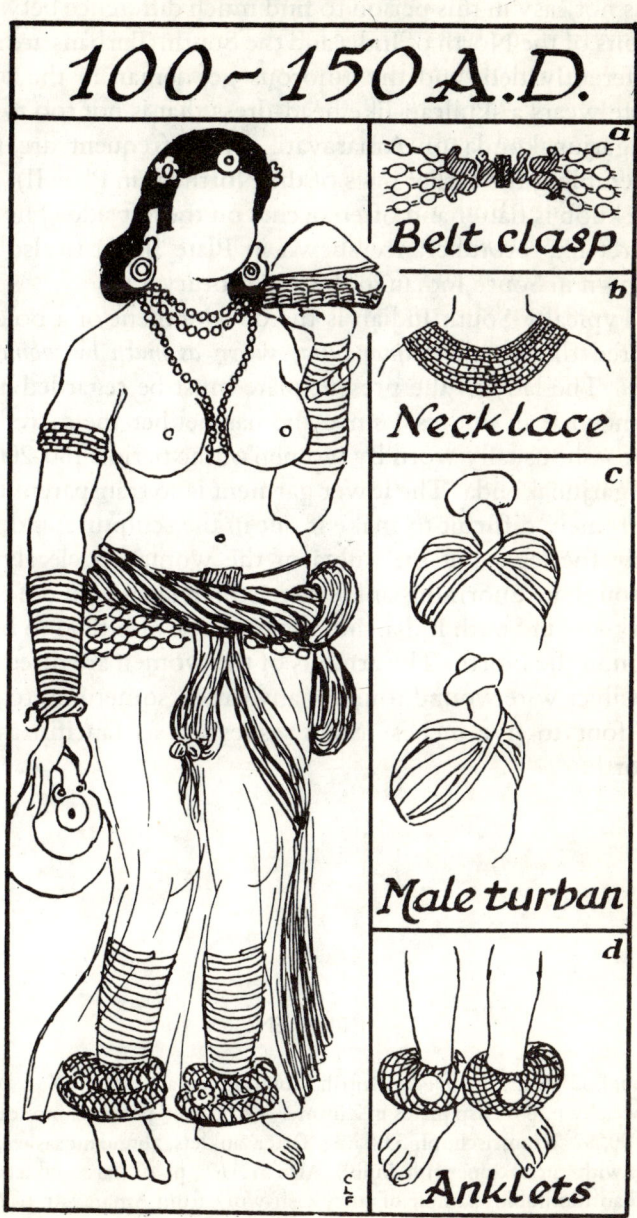

PLATE IV

It is not easy in this period to find much difference between the habits of the North of India and the South. Turbans are slightly differently tied, and the amorous gentleman in the opposite plate wears a skullcap-like head-dress that is not too typical of Nagarjunakonda or Amaravati. More frequent are turbans resembling the earlier ones of the North (as in Plate II), though the knob is flatter and often occurs on the left side. The kind of turret-like protuberance shewn in Plate III (c) is also widely known in South Indian in the 2nd century A.D.

Typically South Indian is the development of a bold, thick sacred thread, the *yajnopavita*, worn *as much by women as by men*. The lady in the present plate must be regarded as being somewhat in undress, since she has neither the sacred thread nor sash, usually worn by women of the period 150-200 A.D. at Nagarjunakonda. The lower garment is so transparent that it is extremely difficult to make it out in the sculpture; indeed, not only the legs, but the vulva of the woman is clearly shewn through it. Enormous anklets are still in fashion in the 2nd century A.D. in South India, and the bracelets also tend to be richer than in the North. The armlets of the women are often of gold or silver wire wound round many times, sometimes to a width of four to five inches. Male sashes are as fanciful as in the North.

REFERENCES

Douglas Barrett, *Amaravati*, British Museum. See also *Marg*, IX, 2, pp. 61-71, especially p. 68. Also plates in Zimmer, 87 ('turret' protuberance of turbans) pl. 90, 92. Kramrisch, pl. 33 (large 'fetter' anklets, abundant sashes, one turban with 'turret', one with 'bulb'). Also in *AIP.*, pl. 67 (large anklets, sashes), and an admirable example of fancy sash-work from Amaravati, pl. 75.

PLATE IV
150 – 200 A.D.

South India

PLATE V

A prince or nobleman of Northern India. The drapery of the *dhoti* is more generous, the sash or waistband seems to be abandoned, but a mass of folds is gathered between the legs in front. The new addition is a cloak, a *chadar*, a piece of cloth worn in a variety of ways, thrown across one or both shoulders, allowed to fall over an arm, or with one end hanging at the back or front. An identical loose piece of drapery is worn by women, see Plate VI. Similar *chadars* occur at Mathura.

The turban shews great variety, though generally speaking it is more tightly wound and less voluminous than in the previous centuries. Many patterned cloths are used, often with jewellery inserted. The fan-shaped *turra* end, crest-like, much worn now by Pathans and Panjabis, occurs in Gandhara, see inset *c*. (But this is genuine Indian fashion, for the foreigners wear Central Asian caps, not reproduced here.)

Necklaces and breast ornaments are both worn, but are not too elaborate in this century; armlets are tied with what appear to be strings and the bracelets are simple.

Sandals, a foreign fashion, are worn by Indian noblemen on occasion, but rarely (inset *d*).

REFERENCES

Zimmer, pl. 63, 64. Rowland, pl. 35, 37 (the prince and lady in right bottom corner), pl. 45 (an early Bodhisattva dressed in the same manner). *AIP.*, pl. 114 (the adorants of the Buddha, on the left of the flame-enveloped figure, are all in similar dress), pl. 22 for examples of jewellery of the time. Numerous examples in Foucher's *L'art greco-bouddhique du Gandhara*. Some in J. Ph. Vogel's La sculpture de Mathura (*Ars Asiatica*, Paris).

PLATE V
200-300 A.D.

a Breast ornament
b Armlet
c Turban
d Sandal

PLATE VI

Dress of Northern Indian lady of quality. As during many hundreds of years, the difference between the attire of males and females, with the possible exception of the headgear and jewellery, is almost nil. Even in the case of the latter the difference is hardly noticeable, for men wear almost identical earrings, necklaces, and bracelets, the main difference being in the turbans and anklets. The enormous 'fetter' anklets for women of the 2nd century continue into the beginnings of the 3rd; but disappear towards the end. Metal belts are worn more sparingly by women, the garment now being held up by a mere string, as the sari is today. The example in inset *b* is from Mathura.

There is a variety of head-covering, of which two are shewn in the plate opposite. The type shewn in the main figure and in inset *c* is of Western Asian origin, but is wide-spread in Northern India in the 3rd century A.D. Flowing ribbons at the back are typical of Iranian headgear (the so-called 'Sasanian ribbon'). The perky little bow on the top of the head in inset *a* is from an ivory of Mathura origin found at Begram, Afghanistan, and there are a number of ways in which it can be tied, always on the top of the crown.

It must be mentioned that peplum-like Greco-Roman dresses, with western Asiatic variations, were worn by upper class women in most parts of Northern India from Kabul in Afghanistan to Mathura in U.P. Because they were 'foreign' fashions, they are omitted in this book yet they were worn for at least six hundred years by numbers of Indian women. The suggestion has been made that the modern sari has developed from the Greco-Roman *peplos*. I can find no evidence whatever for that hypothesis. Cp. Plate XXIX of this book. In any case the peplos was a *sewn* garment.

REFERENCES

- As for the previous plate. Also Rowland, pl. 36, 37 (rightmost figure), 49 (*a*) (foreign dress at Mathura), pl. 51 (ivory engravings from Begram) *Marg*, IX, 2, p. 37, pl. 2 (the female adorants in foreign costume).

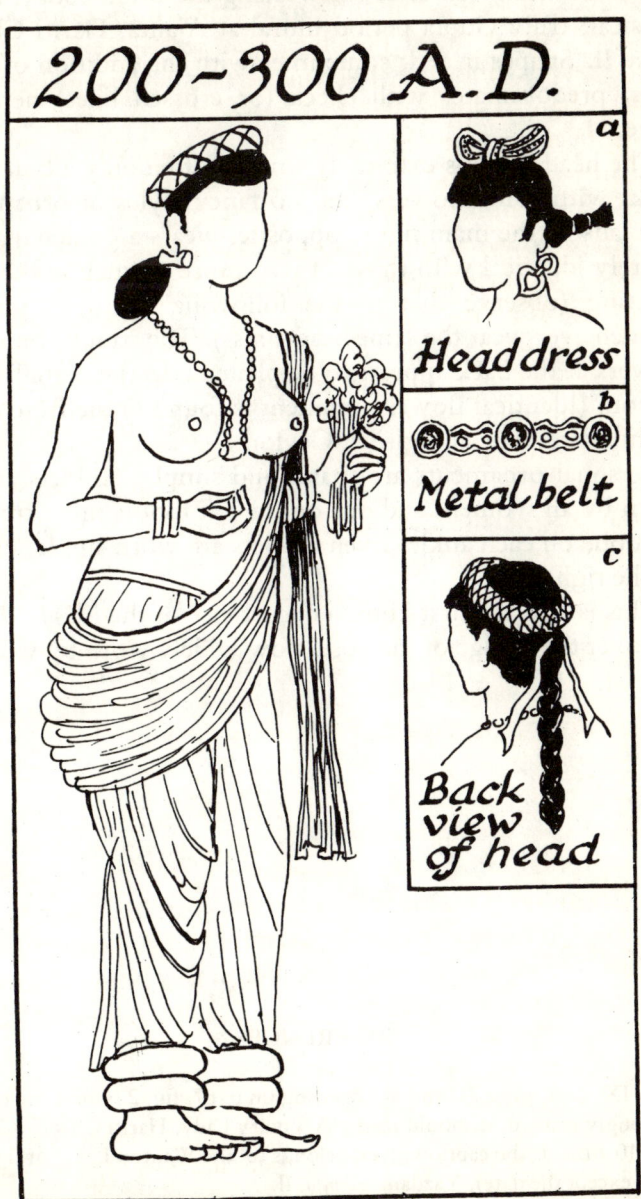

PLATE VII

The 'Maharashtrian style' of wearing the dhoti today, in the classical, truly Gupta period mural at Ajanta, Hariti Chapel, Cave II. Stripes in red, sometimes with the addition of black lines, predominate, with check (or crossed lines) here and there.

The head dress is extremely simple; often only a bun at the back, with some flowers, and no fancy styles or ornaments. The lady in the main figure opposite, wears a golden diadem, entirely identical with those of two more women in the same painting (observe that in the following centuries no two women ever wear the same head-dress). The strange bundle of flowers at the back appears to be plaited into the pigtail with a ribbon. (Identical flower ornament is found in the frescos of a slightly later date at Sigiriya, Ceylon.)

Personal ornaments are sparse and simple. Anklets are not worn by all women, and one on the left foot is more frequent than one on each ankle. Even armlets are worn single, usually on the right arm.

This is also the first known occurrence of the *baindi*, the red dot over the bridge of the nose, now widely worn by women.

REFERENCES

Marg, IX, I, pl. page 74, and my drawing on p. 67, fig. 2 (where the caption is wrongly printed; it should read : 'A Votary Lady, Hariti Chapel, Cave II, 400-410 A.D.', as the caption given belongs to 'the Wanton Lady' of figure 7. p. 69, except the date), Yazdani, *Ajanta*, II.

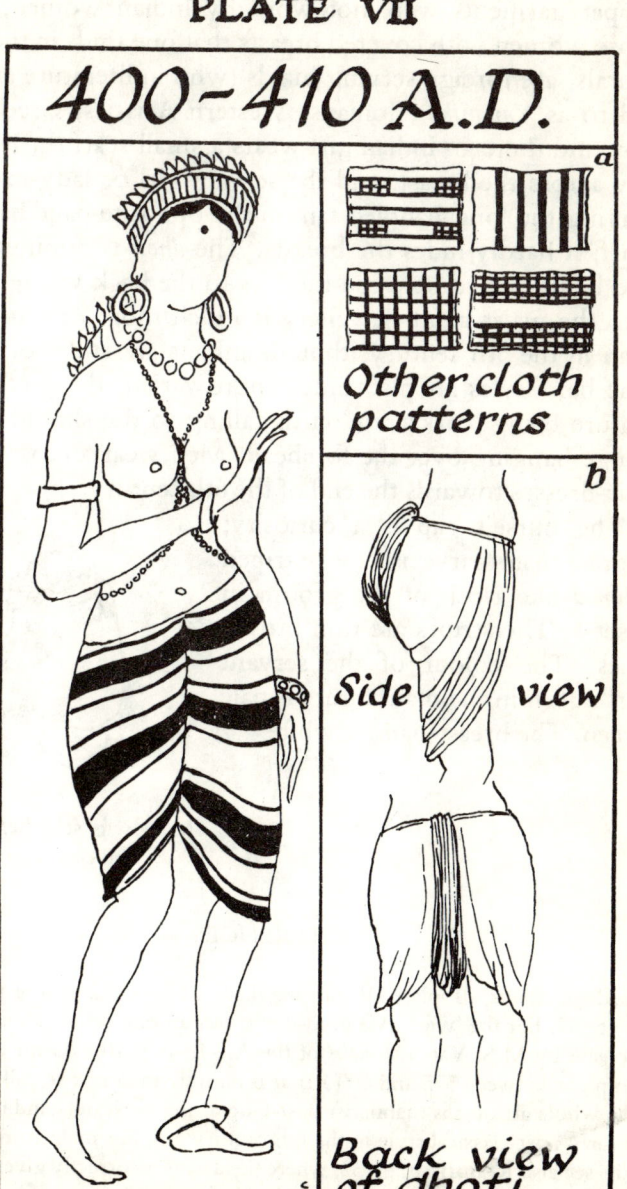

PLATE VIII

Upper garments were not worn by Indian women, and all those women with covered breasts that one finds in the Ajanta murals, are foreign serving maids (who in literature are referred to as *Yavanikas*, Ionians, Western Asiatics, Greeks). But here and there an Indian girl wears a small scarf thrown casually across the breast, and the servant girl or lady-in-waiting waving the long-handled fan on the opposite page has such a scarf; it hardly hides the breasts. The *dhoti* is diminutive, the end being pulled between the legs to the back where it is tied into the waist-band. Jewellery is much more rich and varied than in the 5th century, though anklets are still worn singly. The hair-styles are also much more varied, the predominant feature being 'corkscrew' curls falling to the shoulders and a fringe hanging over the forehead. **Men wear almost wig-like hair-dresses towards the end of the 6th century.**

The nurse's cap is a curiosity; more customary is the striped *tahmad*-like cloth of the groom in inset *b*. The stripes are thin brown lines. The colour of the servant girl's *dhoti* in the main figure is pale green. The breast-band is white.

Male 'wig' style head-dress: 6th century A.D.

REFERENCES

Yazdani, *Ajanta*, III, plate LII and elsewhere. *Marg*, IX, 2, colour plate opposite p. 87. For the 'wig' style head-dress, see, among others : *The Temple at Deogarh* by M.S. Vats (*Memoirs* of the A.S.I., No. 70). As the date of this temple is between 575 and 600 A.D it is entirely incorrect to call it 'Gupta'. The whole art of it is mannerist post-Gupta. the most outstanding example of early post-classical style in the 6th century A.D. For male attire and 'wig' hair, see also Kramrisch, pl. 52, where the date is incorrectly given as 'About 500'. It should be 'end of 6th century'.

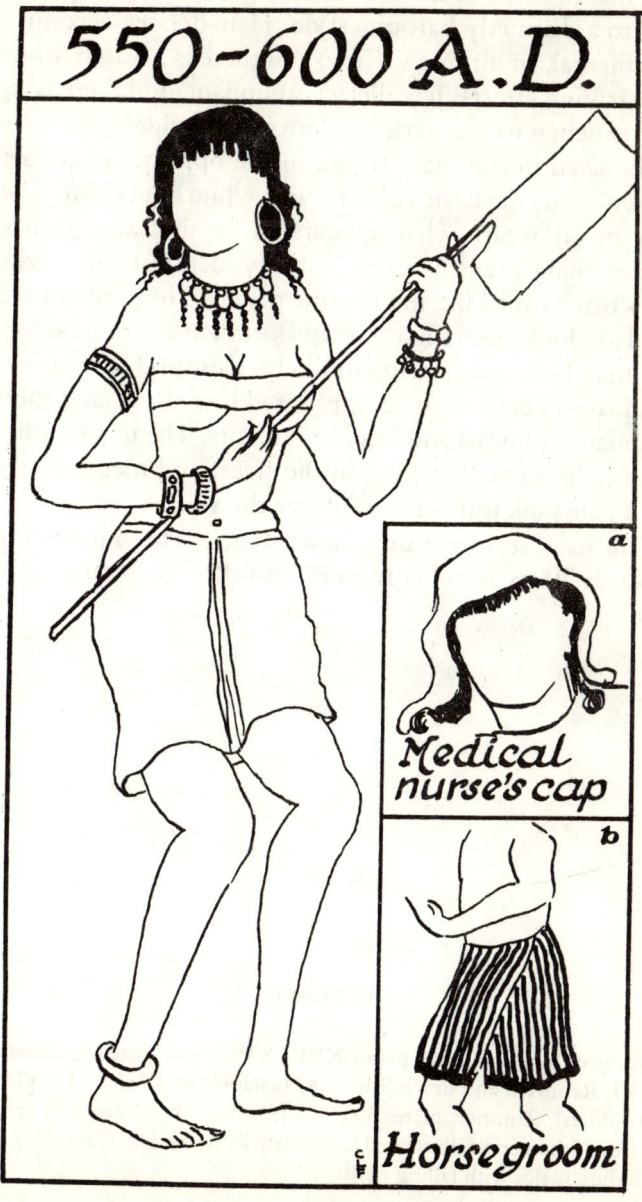

PLATE IX

The mannerisms of the 6th century gradually give place, in the 7th, to a distinctly baroque style. Hair-dresses become highly ornamental, of infinite variety, and there is a search for unusual and striking effects. Jewellery is abundant, and there is a growing tendency to use varied colours. The widely-spaced stripes in the *dhoti* in the main figure in the opposite plate, are deep brown while the basic colour is not white but cream. The royal lady in (*a*) wears what appears to be shot silk (*moirée*), the stripes being greyish-green (entirely identical coloured stripes are worn by the king in the same panel). The garment worn by this lady looks more like a sewn skirt than a *dhoti* or sarong, but this may be taken as being unlikely. Gold and silver ornaments and flowers bedeck the complicated hair-dress, and there is an abundance of pearl and bead ornaments. The main figure in the plate (a 'princess' walking in the street and meeting a beggar) has a pale pink muslin scarf above the waist.

The 'halo' style coiffure, shewn in inset *b* becomes fashionable towards 700 A. D. and continues into the 8th century. (Cp Plate XI).

REFERENCES

Madanjeet Singh, *Ajanta*, plates XVII, XVIII, etc. Yazdani, *Ajanta*, III, pl. LXVI. Rambach and de Golish : *The Golden Age of Indian Art*, plates 47-48 (no anklets). Zimmer, plates 300, 301 (for 'halo' head-dress). Typical head-dresses of the period illustrated in my article, *Marg*, IX, 1, figs. 5, 6, 7 and 8, including males with falling curls.

PLATE X

The baroque love for romantic novelty and rich variation did not exclude the male. Extravagant and curious hair-styles are the rule, the hair often being piled up in a bun or coif that can only be described as effeminate; crowns, diadems and jewelled ornaments are worn with relish in the hair, on the neck and even round the waist. This waistband is short-lived, though charateristic of the century, especially in Northern India and even as far South as Pattadakal, Chalukya country. It is not worn by the king in the so-called 'portrait' of King Mahendravarman (inset picture *b* on opposite page) in the Adi Varaha Cave, Mamallapuram (about 650 A.D.). The strange coiffure in (*a*) is from Ellura (*minus* a crown), and is of the same period. The sacred thread (*yajnopavita*) is widely worn also by women. Earrings tend to be enormous.

REFERENCES

Zimmer, plates 301, 302, 231 and 233. Rambach and de Golish, *The Golden Age*, plates 39, 40, 44, 45, 46 (the main figure in my plate is a composite one).

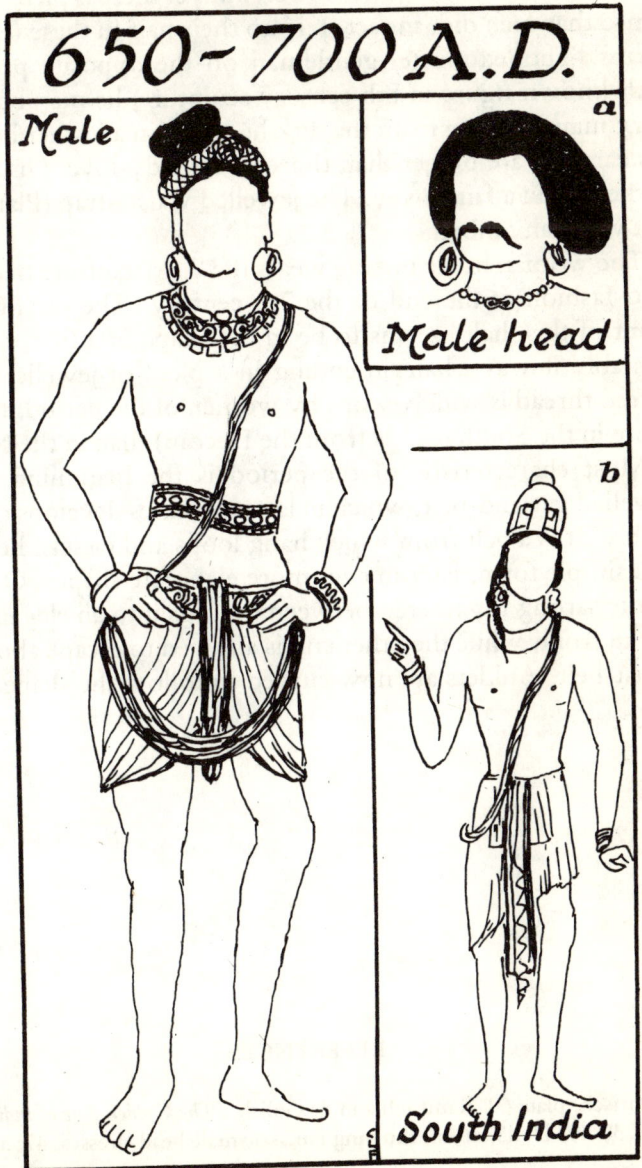

PLATE XI

The kind of baroque fancy hair-do that men show in the middle of the 8th century is hard to credit; yet there is pictorial evidence that men did, in fact, pile up their hair in these feminine forms. The 'exquisite' gentleman on the opposite page is a well-known figure in 8th century sculpture; he may be a military man, judging from the dirk he wears in a leather belt, but his earrings are bigger than those of his lady-love. His *dhoti* is tucked up in a fancy way. The jewelled waist-strap (Plate X) is not worn any more.

The woman in the picture wears the 'halo' coiffure that came into fashion at the end of the 7th century. The ornament in front of this 'halo' seems to be in the shape of a fir cone; presumably it was a hairpin ending in a piece of jewellery. The sacred thread is widely worn by women of the period, though more in the South (this is from the Deccan) than in the North.

Most characteristic of the period is the beginning of the jewelled garland-belt, which in later centuries develops considerably. It is a belt from which hang loops and tassels, here still in a simple form, later in ever more elaborate shapes. One end of the sarong is gathered between the legs into an elegant border in front, while the other end is allowed to escape above the waist-belt. Anklets are now curved to follow the shape of the foot.

REFERENCES

Kramrisch, plate 69. Rambach and de Golish : *The Golden Age of Indian Art*, plates 39-40, 43, 45, 46, all showing fantastic male head-dresses, 47, 52.

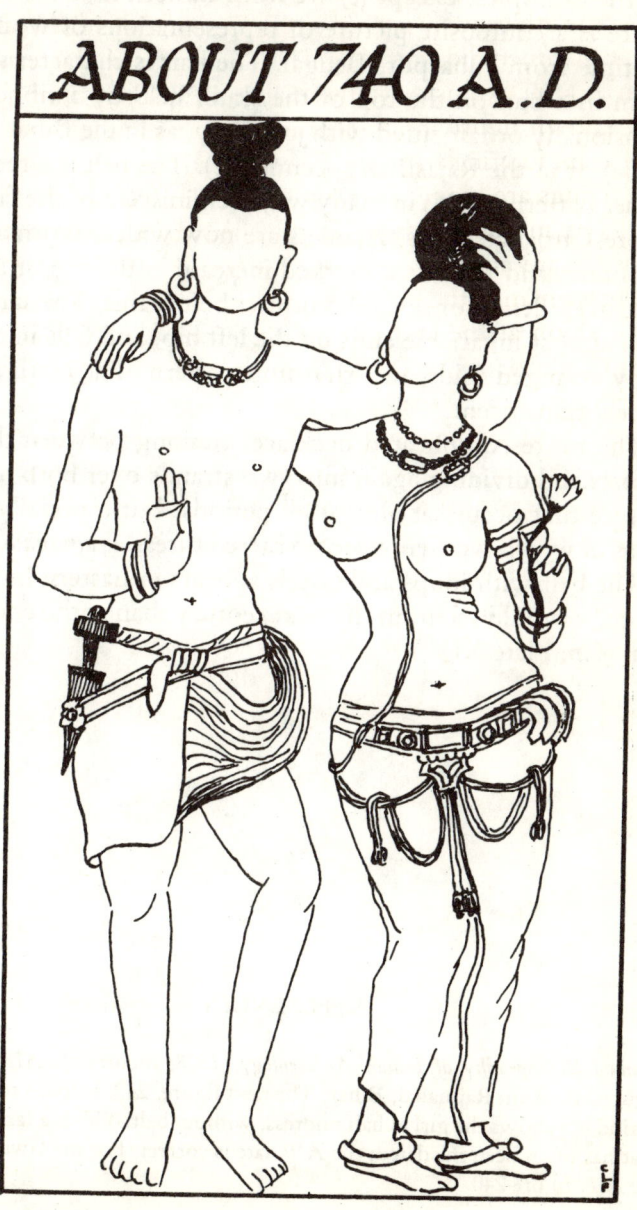

PLATE XII

All the examples, except (*e*) are from Eastern India. The main figure is a composite picture of representations of women of the time from Paharpur, Bengal. The hair is characteristically worn in a bun on the top of the skull, held by a ribbon and occasionally ornamented with jewellery, as in the Bihar example (*a*) or in the Rajasthan specimen (*e*). The belt is a return to earlier patterns and is in many ways reminiscent of the fashions of pre-Christian times. Armlets are now widely worn and are elaborate; and there is a marked increase in the use of a scarf, little in evidence for several centuries before this. The sarong or *dhoti* almost invariable ends on the left hip, and falls in charmingly arranged folds, in a rhythmic pattern. The cloth is thin, almost translucent.

The more complicated necklace, running between the two breasts and dividing again into two strands over both hips is a feature that occurs at almost all periods, but especially in the areas in which women wore no sacred thread (*yajnopavita*).

The belt with loops and tassels appears in Eastern India, but more, it would seem, in the next century than at the end of the 9th. (Cp. Plate XIV.)

REFERENCES

Annual Bibliography of Indian Archaeology, 1928, incorrect). *AIP.*, pl. 37, figure 241, from Rajmahal, Bihar. The next figure, 242, belongs to the same period but shows the girl in half undress, without belt. This is a famous piece that has often been misdated; the *AIP* date is correct. For the Gwalior head, see *AIP*. figure 240.

PLATE XII

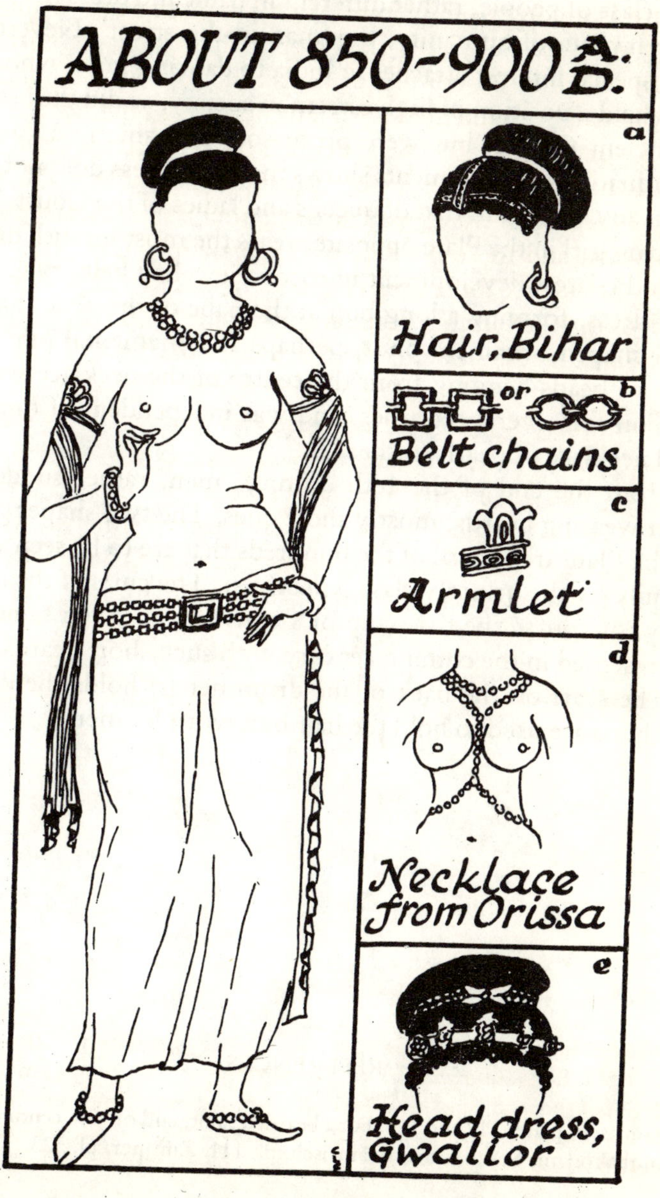

ABOUT 850-900 A.D.

a. Hair, Bihar
b. Belt chains
c. Armlet
d. Necklace from Orissa
e. Head dress, Gwalior

PLATE XIII

Admittedly, musicians and dancing women belong to a distinct class of people, rather different in habit and dress from the ordinary run of humanity, the 'man-in-the-street'. Nevertheless, special interest attaches in India to dancing girls, who not only held a position of high esteem in society, as did the *hetaera* in ancient Greece, but were precursors of fashion. A careful examination of monuments shows that their dress does not differ in any way from that of queens and ladies of the Court. The dancing girl in the Plate opposite wears the most modish dress, with the latest development in rococo jewelled belt-style. The hair-dress, forming a long bun at the nape of the neck, has an oval-shaped ornament on it, perhaps an ornamental pin. The row of beads hanging from the centre of the necklace was in fashion for several centuries, and was independent of the second necklace of pearls (or beads).

From the end of the 10th century, men, rather suddenly, start wearing beards, mostly short ones. The two shapes given in the Plate are typical of the hundreds that are to be seen worn mainly by the princely class (*kshatriyas*). The curls of the beard may, of course, be the sculptor's convention. Even saints are represented in the coming century with such short beards.

The scarf on the back of the drummer (*c*) holds the drum. Ribbons are used to hold the hair bun worn by men.

REFERENCES

Kramrisch, plates 117 and 118. For a bearded saint, end of 10th century, from Kumbakonam, South India, Kramrisch, pl. 111. Zimmer, pl. 323.

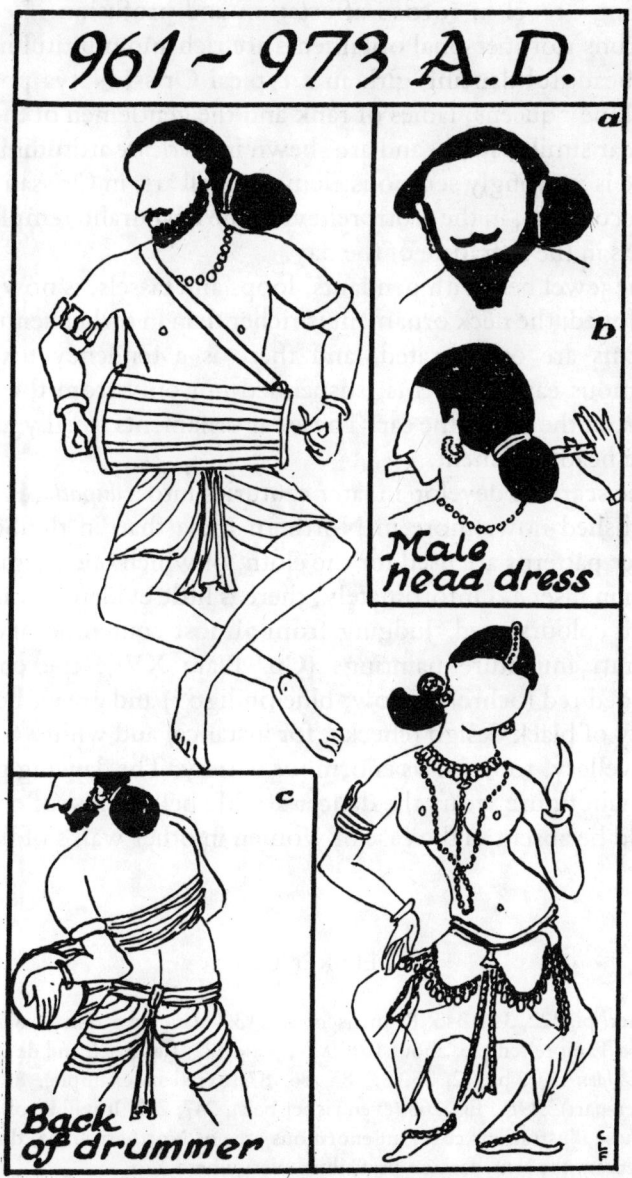

PLATE XIV

Around 1000 A.D. fashions—like literature and sculpture and painting—revel in rococo affectation and profusion. Decoration runs riot, personal ornaments are rich and multitudinous. The beautiful dancing girl, in a typical Orissi Natya pose, is not alone : queens, ladies of rank and the gentlemen of the day all wear similar attire, and are shewn in *précieuse* attitudinizing. There is a strongly sensuous element in all art, in Orissan temple decoration, in the erotic relievi of the Khajuraho temples, as well as in the literature of the day.

The jewel belt with pendants, loops and tassels, is now fully developed; the neck ornament is richer than in earlier centuries, diadems are complicated, and there is a tendency towards enormous ear ornaments, suspended not only from the lobe, but from the top of the ear. These ear ornaments usually jut out of the head ornament.

The scarf, to develop in later centuries into a *dupatta*, is well-established now, more in Northern India than in the South. Clever patterns are used for the cloth, of which one example is given in inset *a*. Unfortunately, there is little evidence available of the colours used. Judging from almost contemporary Jain Gujarati miniature paintings (Cp. Plate XVI), the colours included red (ochre), yellow, blue (indigo ?) and green, besides plenty of black design (checks, for instance) and white.

Jewellery, too, shows enormous variety. The dancing girl in the main figure wears the dancer's ankle bells. This, of course, would be absent in the case of women in other walks of life.

REFERENCES

Zimmer, pl. 322, 344, 345, Kramrisch, pl. 113, a dancing girl in a wall painting in a Tanjore temple, about 1010 A.D., plate 122. Rambach and de Golish, *The Golden Age*, pl. 72, 75, 83, 85, 86, 87 (excellent example), 88 (male counter-part). *AIP.*, fig. 268 (even richer belt), 247, 249. It will be observed that these illustrations cover an enormous area of Northern India, down to the Deccan, the same fashion prevailing everywhere.

PLATE XIV

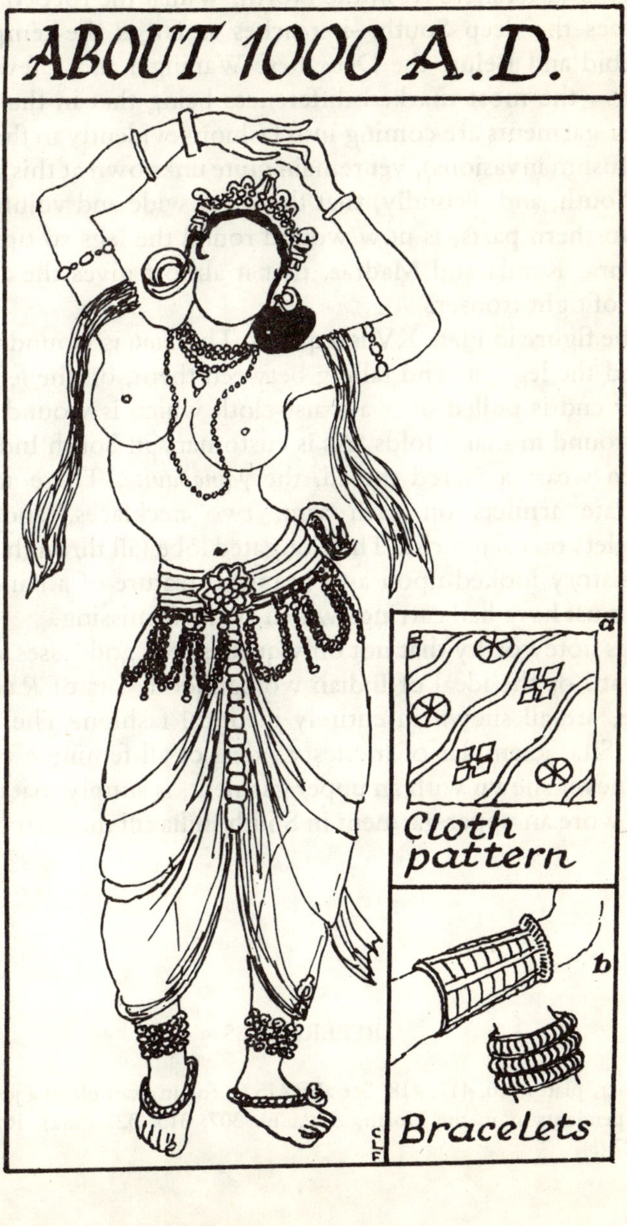
ABOUT 1000 A.D.
a
Cloth pattern
b
Bracelets

PLATE XV

In about 1100 A.D. South India shows, for the first time, distinct regional differences from the North. Whilst the rococo hardly touches the deep South—it reaches as far as the temples of Halebid and Belur, the Deccanese Warangal and a few other places—the most marked differences being that in the North upper garments are coming into fashion (evidently in the wake of Muslim invasions), yet remain quite unknown at this time in the South; and secondly, that the *dhoti*, wide and voluminous in Northern parts, is now wound round the legs so tightly in Andhra, Kerala and Madras, that it almost gives the appearance of tight trousers.

The figure in Plate XV is a queen. The *dhoti* is wound tightly round the legs, its end falling between them, on the left. The other end is pulled over a waist-cloth which is wound round and round in many folds. As is customary in South India, the queen wears a sacred thread, the *yajnopavita*. There are two separate armlets on each arm, two necklaces, and three bracelets on each wrist. The elongated lobe (all through Indian art history looked upon as a beautiful feature of a handsome ear) must have had earrings which are now missing.

It is noteworthy that not only queens, but goddesses such as Parvati, or the ideal of Indian womanhood, Sita of *Ramayana* fame, are all shewn in entirely identical fashion. The reason why Sita, exemplar of modesty, ideal of all feminine virtues, was never shewn with an upper garment, is simply that no one ever wore an upper garment in South India till modern times.

REFERENCES

Zimmer, plates 416, 417, 418. See also 415 (*a*) for an example of a jewel belt with pendants as in the North. *AIP*., pl. 307, 313, 327 (Sita). Rowland, pl. 127 (*b*).

PLATE XV
ABOUT 1100 A.D.

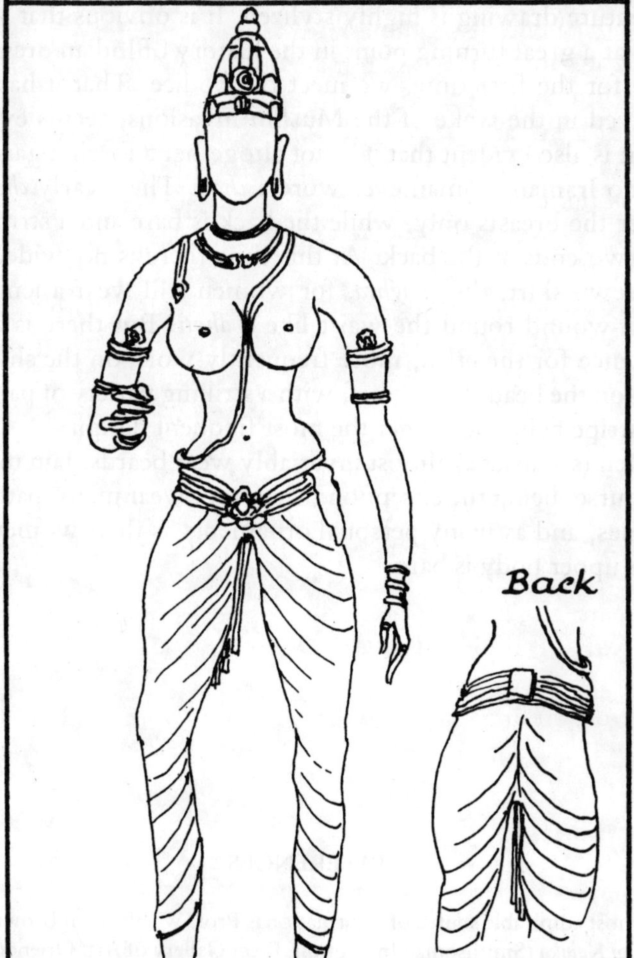

Back

South India

PLATE XVI

The manuscript from which the main figure is taken is dated 1127 A.D. and is one of many from Gujarat. Presumably, the dress shewn with such attention to detail was worn some time before the date of the manuscript and some time after. The miniature drawing is highly stylized. It is obvious that we are here at a great turning point in the history of Indian dress : for here for the first time, we meet the bodice. That it has been evolved in the wake of the Muslim invasions, seems evident; but it is also evident that it is not altogether a foreign garment, for no Iranian woman ever wore a *choli*. These early *cholis* all cover the breasts only, while the back is bare and a string ties the two ends at the back. At this time there is no evidence of the sewn skirt, the *ghaghra*, for women still wear a length of cloth wound round the waist like a *dhoti*. But there is ample evidence for the *orhni*, more frequently worn on the shoulder than on the head. It is a scarf, with a striking variety of patterns, the stripe being no longer the most frequent design.

Men (see inset *a*) almost invariably wear beards, Jain monks, of course, being the exception. Men, too, wear many-patterned textiles, and as many personal ornaments as their women, but their upper body is bare.

REFERENCES

The most admirable source of information is Prof. W. Norman Brown's *The Story of Kalaka* (Smithsonian Institution, Freer Gallery of Art, Oriental Series No. 1, Washington, 1933) and Prof. Brown's many other contributions. See especially figs. 2, 4 and 6 in *Kalaka*. Fine manuscripts of almost the same time in the Bharatiya Vidya Bhavan, Bombay. Only slightly later is Rowland, pl. 130.

PLATE XVII

The queen of the Chola dynasty shews every sign of the rich ornamentation that comes with the rococo. Two hundred years after the women in the North had begun to wear bodices, she still appears, however, bare from the waist up. This is the second divergence from the North; the other is the tightly wrapped *dhoti*, a speciality of South India never seen in the North.

But the looped belt, now highly elaborate, is identical with northern fashions; and even in the design of the cloth one can discern similarities with patterns worn in Gujarat and Rajasthan. In inset *a* the second stripe pattern is identical with similar rosette designs in Gujarat, and the lowermost ribbon design is found, in a simpler form, in the earlier *dhoti* in Plate XIV, Orissa. The Chola lady wears no scarf. The curving anklet, made to fit the shape of the foot, is identical in North and South. The head-dress too shows much similarity to northern hair fashions of the same period.

REFERENCES

Archaeological Survey of India photograph No. 465/1948, from the Chingleput District of Madras. *AIP.*, fig. 321. Cp. also 320.

PLATE XVII

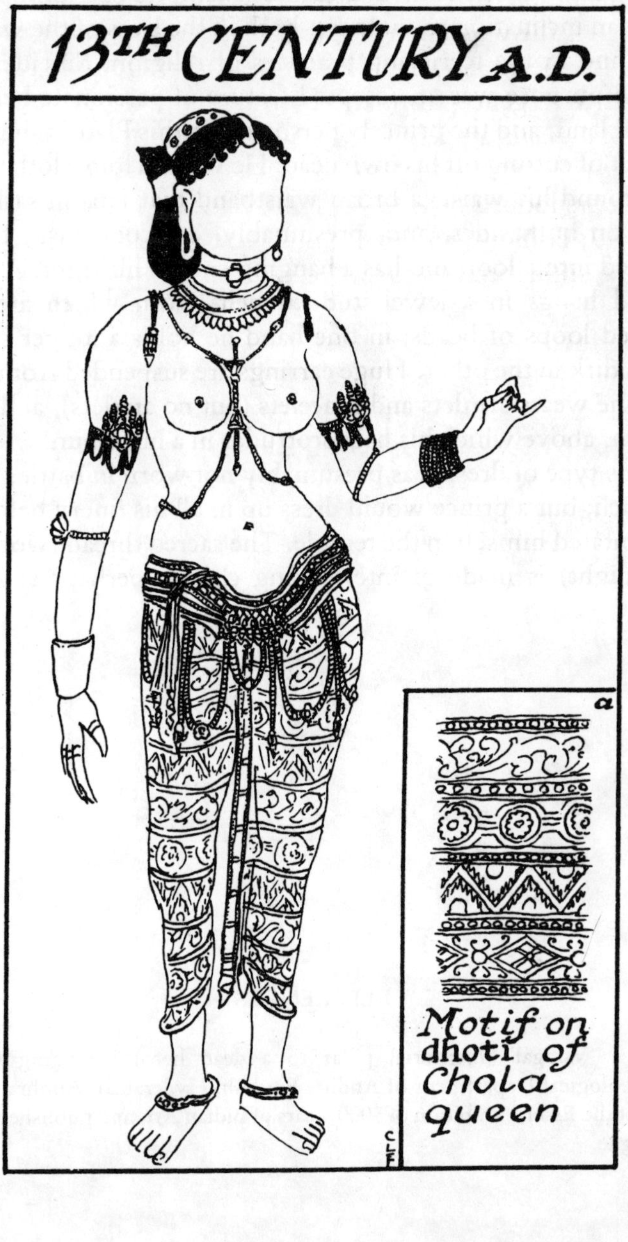
13TH CENTURY A.D.
a
Motif on dhoti of Chola queen
CLF

PLATE XVIII

In South India, from prehistoric times onwards, there was a strong martial element. The earliest examples of Tamil poetry shew an inclination to violence, both in the lives of the warrior class and in the terrifying practices of religion. Suicide for a sacred purpose was an accepted feature of passionate belief in Tamil land, and the princely personage in this Plate is shewn in the act of cutting off his own head. He wears a loin-cloth wrapped round his waist, a broad waistband that falls in sash-like ends on both sides, and, presumably, a second sash, that is formed into a loop and has a hanging end on his right. A short sword hangs in a jewel-studded belt, from which are suspended loops of beads; in one hand he holds a longer sword and a dirk in the other. Huge earrings are suspended from both ears, he wears armlets and bracelets (but no anklets), and has a crown, above which his hair protrudes in a huge bun.

This type of dress was presumably not worn in battle, being too rich; but a prince would dress up in all his finery before he decapitated himself in the temple. The sacred thread (worn day and night) is made of interlocking chains, perhaps silver or gold.

REFERENCES

From a 'Viragal' (memorial pillar to a dead hero) belonging to the Archaeological Department of Andhra Pradesh, Hyderabad, Andhra. Exhibited at the Essen exhibition of 5000 Years of Indian Art, and published in the catalogue.

PLATE XVIII

14TH CENTURY A.D.

PLATE XIX

The evidence for costumes worn at the court of the Timurids is so rich that only a few examples will be shewn here. So strong was the feeling for fashion in this aristocratic society that pictures illustrating the times of previous reigns adhere carefully to the dress worn in those earlier days, even if the painting was done in the next reign or later. Realism is the keynote of these records of the doings of a noble dynasty.

The main figure shows one of the many portraits of Babar himself (1526-1530 A.D.). While here he is wearing a white coat, in others he would wear one that was buff-coloured, when the boots would be green. These high boots were worn when riding; while the smaller shoes shewn in the inset were for the home or the camp. A long-sleeved garment, a kind of shirt, in a completely different colour, was worn near the body, under the short-sleeved coat, and the lapel of the coat was sometimes of gold cloth. But there was much less luxury than in later days. The whole dress is patently unsuited for India's climate and was imported from the cold highlands of Central Asia.

Turbans are much more voluminous than in later Mughal days, and are wound round a clearly visible *kula* (a kind of pointed skull-cap) which is sometimes very tall, even in Humayun's days (1530-40 and 1555-56).

The attendant wore an almost uniform-like dress, as shewn in (*b*), in contrasting colours, with the coat ending in two or three flaps hanging from the waist, and a much longer one at the rear. This dress continues for men-at-arms into Humayun's reign. The dress is, as a rule, without any pattern, but turbans sometimes have stripes or checks.

REFERENCES

Mughal Miniatures, Lalit Kala Akademi, 1955, pl. 1, 2, 3. Stchoukine (see Bibliography).

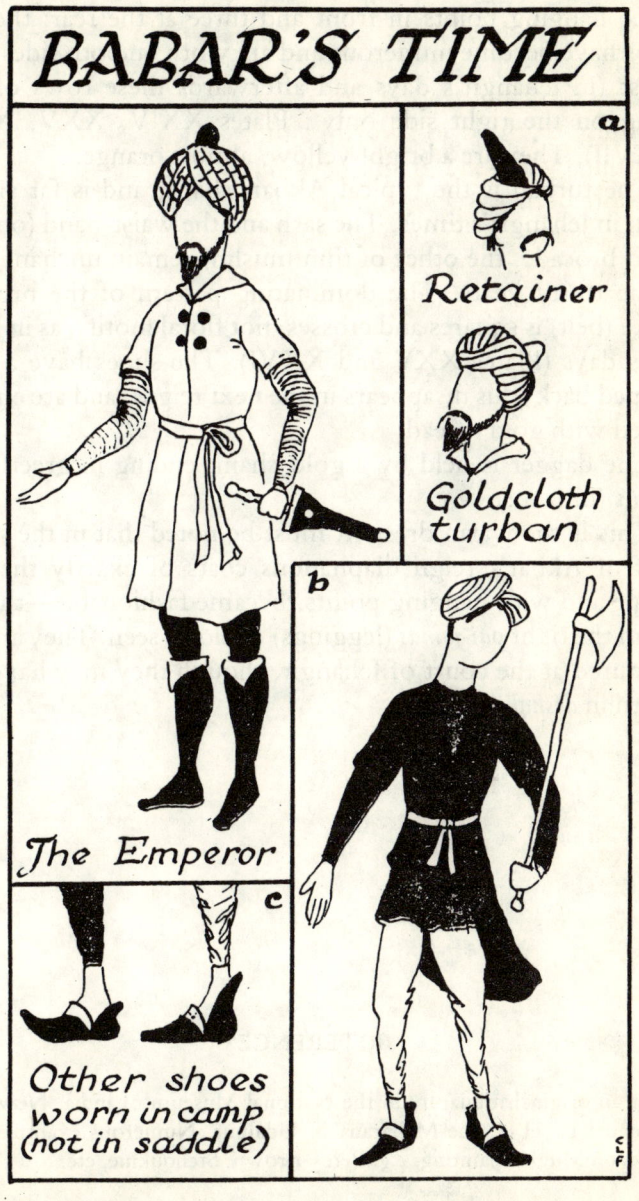

PLATE XX

A gentleman at Akbar's court (about 1600). The violet coat has three hanging points in front and three at the rear; the lapel flaps have become numerous and are worn on both sides of the chest (in Jehangir's days and afterwards these rows of flaps hang on the right side only : Plates XXIV, XXV, XXVI, XXVII). They are a bright yellow, almost orange.

The turban is the typical Akbari shape, and is far simpler than in Jehangir's times. The sash and the waist-band (one is of gold brocade, the other of thin muslin) remain unchanged for some thirty years. The dominating pattern of the brocaded *patka* (belt) is squares and crosses, not floral motifs, as in Jehangir's days (Plates XXV and XXVI). The shoes have a horn-shaped back (this disappears in the next reign), and are embroidered with gold thread.

The dagger is held by a gold chain, ending in green pompoms (or jade?).

This is the warm dress. It must be noted that in the second half of Akbar's reign diaphanous coats of exactly the same shape and with hanging points, became fashionable—through them the tight *pai-jamas* (leggings) could be seen. They are little favoured at the court of Jehangir, though they may have been worn in *déshabille*.

REFERENCES

After an original miniature in the National Museum of India. New Delhi, presented by H.H. the Maharana of Udaipur. Numerous examples in all books on Mughal painting. *e.g.* Percy Brown, Stchoukine, etc.

PLATE XX
AKBAR'S COURT

PLATE XXI

The Plate shews the less aristocratic members of Akbar's court (1556-1605) : a maid, a palace servant, people of the street.

The maid offering a cup of wine (about 1580) wears the fashionable frock ending in sharp points that hang down from the hem of the skirt. Four such points were in fashion earlier (as in the case of the palace servant opposite, about twenty years earlier), but by this time there were six. This is a shirt made of an opaque material, and the young woman's decorated sash hangs underneath it, the ends being visible in front of the tight, bright red trousers. Where the shirt opens, from the neck downwards along the V-shaped slit, hangs on one side a number of braid-like loops. This remains modish for a long time and develops into rows of long flaps. The thin, diaphanous *orhni* (head-kerchief) is still short, but will become longer in the next century.

Pompoms and tassels are beginning to be worn, both on shoes and where the jewellery is tied, *e.g.* on the bracelet.

The palace servant has four buttons on both sides of his chest,—there were two in Babar's and Humayun's 'uniform', —and a simple *patka* (sash), into which his dagger is tucked and held by two small chains. The turban is typical of Akbar's days with a tight front bundle and a bold slope backwards, the *tula* of Humayun's times not being worn any more.

REFERENCES

AIP pl. 125, fig. 640. Wilkinson, *Mughal Painting*, (Faber Gallery, London, 1948), pl. 4, for several palace attendants in similar dress and a variety of colour.

PLATE XXII

It is once again important to observe that Islamic court fashions, under Akbar, as well as afterwards, exercised considerable influence on masculine wear among the Hindu upper and middle classes, but hardly any on that of the women. The 16th century Rajasthani fashions of the men are almost identical with those worn in the courts at Agra, Lahore and Delhi. Even the typical Lover, the Nayaka, is dressed *à la Mogul*, with a shirt ending in points, and the low Akbari *pagri* (turban) on his head. Towards the end of the 16th century, when diaphanous *jamas* and skirts became the fashion at court, the gentlemen of Rajasthan wore the same dress. (This went out of fashion around 1610, when transparent skirts were worn only by entertainers, whilst gentlemen and ladies wore opaque material.) The hanging flaps on the chest were worn on both sides (see previous Plate) and the sash was varied, though by no means as gorgeous as in the next reign.

Meanwhile, the Hindu women in the rest of Northern India continued wearing their three-piece costume : the skirt, the bodice and the head-kerchief (*ghaghra, choli, orhni*). The bodice sleeve in this period was boldly embroidered, and sometimes the whole bodice was too (at least, the illustrations suggest embroidery rather than printed design); while there was great variety in the textile patterns of the skirt. The great innovation is the pompom, a court fashion that also touched the remoter village woman, and *orhnis* often end in elaborate tassel-work with many pompoms, as in inset (*b*). However, it must be noted that as yet *orhnis* are never tucked into the skirt. That comes later. (Cp. Plate XXIX.)

REFERENCES

Basil Gray, *Rajput Painting* (Faber Gallery, London, 1948), pl. 2 and 3. Basil Gray, *Indian Miniatures* (Cassirer, Oxford, 1951), pl. VI and VII (only slightly later) : *AIP*, colour plate A, and pl. 81, fig. 396 (same date, same dress, same embroidery), and fig. 399 (*b*). *Burlington Magazine*, Febr. 1948. Fig. 17, 18, 19, 20, 21 (the last a Western Indian miniature, identical wear, Krishna dressed in Mughal costume).

PLATE XXII
RAJASTHAN, 1570

a

b

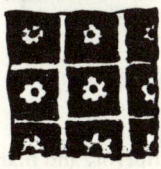
Other patterns on dhotis

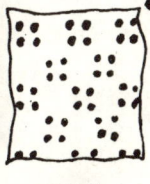

Sleeve of choli in (b)

Village woman

PLATE XXIII

The Emperor in all his glory. The turban, of characteristic shape in this reign, is orange-red; its end, terminating in a gold fringe, is visible on top, above the forehead. Two feathers of some rare bird, presumably bagged by the emperor, are tucked into the turban, and a string of pearls completes the head-dress. (Pearls would not be worn by courtiers.)

The coat is pale cream-coloured silk. (Silk and brocades are worn up to 1668, when Aurangzeb forbids their wear at court.) The trousers are of soft green silk; the shoes, with no horned back and no heels, are of crimson leather, with a plain black piece across the instep.

The waistband has a floral scroll ornament, the flowers being alternately blue and pink; the sash on the other hand is of gold cloth with what appears to be Chinese geometric ornament, within which the centre flowers are again alternately pink and pale blue.

REFERENCES

There are numerous portraits of this art-loving emperor, and many of them are reproduced in books on Mughal painting. This example is a composite picture after three miniature paintings in the National Museum, New Delhi. See Stchoukine (see Bibliography), plates XXI, XXIV, XXVIII.

PLATE XXIII
JAHANGIR c. 1609

PLATE XXIV

Whilst the difference between South Indian and North Indian dress has tended to become marked in the 11th to 13th centuries, in the 17th century in the Deccan we find no marked divergence from the fashions of the North. It is true that for a brief while, around 1570, Deccanese women wore elaborate veils, partially tucked in around the waist, which are surprisingly like the later saris of the North, yet this was a short-lived fashion and had no bearing on the ultimate invention of the modern sari in Northern India arond 1790.

The *Ragamala* miniatures of Bishop Laud, so well datable, give rich evidence of a dress markedly similar to the costumes worn in Rajasthan thirty to fifty years earlier. The Akbari upper garment for men, with hanging points (four or six) is in fashion in the Deccan when no one was wearing it any more in Delhi and Agra; and the small hanging flaps, the Akbari turban and the cross-decorated sash, are modish down South now, during Jehangir's reign.

But Indian women in the Deccan wear the same three-piece dress as is worn by their sisters in the North. Sashes, pompoms and tassels are the craze, and they are complicated, elaborate and varied. Thin transparent muslin *orhnis* are worn on the head, sometimes with polka dots in twos and threes. Mauve and purple are favourite colours. In front, hanging from the waistband, there is an apron-like cloth, a *patka*, lavishly decorated with wavy lines and stripes, usually white, which is much less in evidence in the North.

REFERENCES

Stooke and Khandalavala, *The Laud Ragamala Miniatures* (Cassirer, Oxford, 1953), pl. I, V, X, XIV, XVII, XVIII. Further references will be found in that book.

PLATE XXV

Most of the miniatures of the court shew us the splendours or public receptions and the gala dress of kings and princes, noblemen and petitioners, wearing their 'best'. But the Mughal painters were realists, and so we have also, though in lesser numbers, pictures shewing what the courtiers (nay, even the Emperor) wore on informal occasions, in the seclusion of their private rooms. Prince Khusrau, fat and jovial, leaning against a mighty large bolster, is shewn relaxing in the top of the picture opposite in a white muslin coat.

It seems that the diaphanous muslin dress was *de rigueur* as the fashionable wear at Court for a brief while at the end of Akbar's reign and for a few years after. Jehangir, on the other hand, favoured rich silk and brocades, so that the diaphanous coat went out of fashion for public occasions, to be worn henceforward only by entertainers (dancing girls), as well as by others in the privacy of the home, in the hot weather, as a kind of undress. More research is needed to make these hypotheses acceptable.

The falconer is Khan Alam, in a short jerkin, presumably of leather (falcons have sharp claws), with a row of buttons running down from the neck, arranged in groups of three. There is a decorated sash, and the skirt of the coat reaches about 20 cm. below the belt. The trousers, tapering towards the foot, are of a thick material, and are held in position by a strap under the arch of the foot.

The two examples of designs on sash (*patka*) ends are typical of the floral style of the period. The one under (*a*) is a row of stylized cypresses; the one under (*b*) a much more naturalistic tulip.

REFERENCES

Stchoukine (see Bibliography), Plate XXV.

PLATE XXV
JAHANGIR, c. 1620

Designs on sash ends

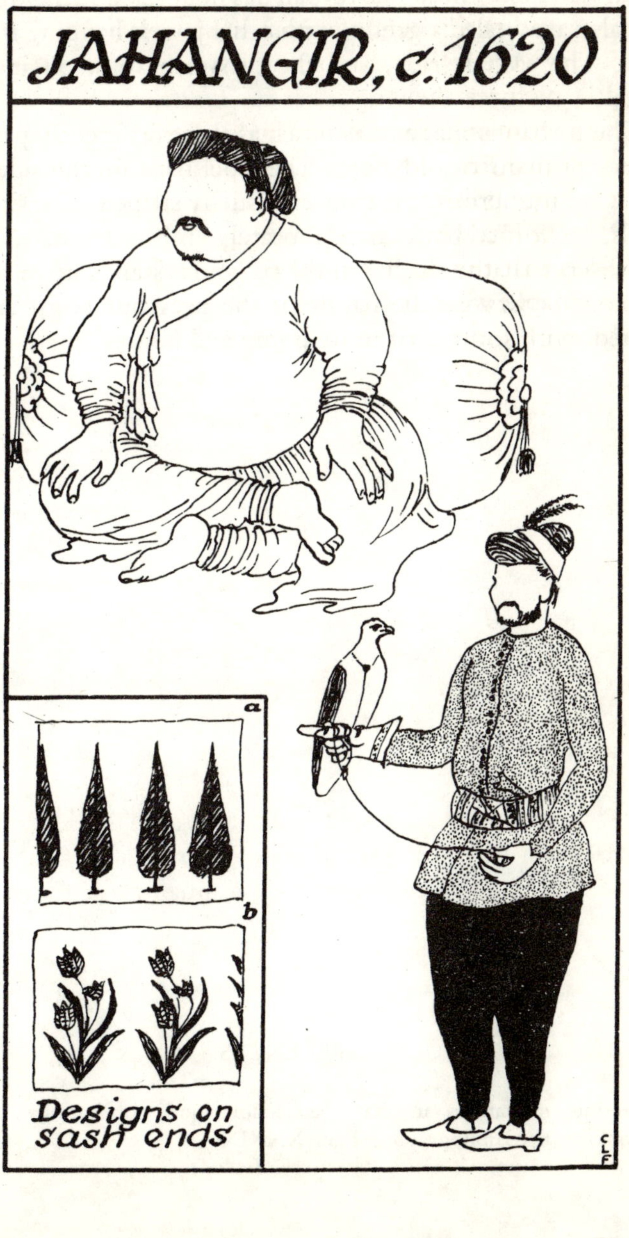

PLATE XXVI

Shahjehan's reign (1627-1659) is marked by more and more luxury and elegance. The turban has not only a string of pearls, but also a jewelled aigrette, with other jewels hanging from the side. The sash is rich, and the ornamentation on it mainly floral.

The turban is made of as much as three differently patterned pieces of mainly gold cloth. The lapel flaps on the side of the chest are numerous, the trousers usually striped. The shoes (no heels, no horned back) are elaborately embroidered.

Observe that the collar of the coat now stands up in military fashion; otherwise the habits of the previous reign are continued, with somewhat more pomp and luxury.

REFERENCES

Numerous miniatures in many collections and publications, See *e.g.* Stchoukine (my Bibliography), Plate XXXIX.

PLATE XXVI
SHAHJEHAN 1640

PLATE XXVII

In the year 1668 the fanatically puritan Emperor Aurangzeb broke with the artistic tradition of his ancestors, sacked all his musicians, got rid of most of his painters, and forbade the wearing of pure silk at Court. Nevertheless, he had many portraits painted of himself.

In many of these he wears a dark green coat, usually with scattered overall pattern, as in the picture opposite. The style is similar to that of the previous reign. The Emperor wears plenty of jewellery (two strings and an aigrette on his turban, pearl bracelets, necklaces, pendants, a jade-handled dagger with a pendant of pearls, rings and armlets.)

The two bottom drawings shew a growing interest in fancy turbans. This continues into the 19th century (see Plate XXX).

REFERENCES

Stchoukine (see Bibliography at end of volume), Plates LII, LIII, LIV. There is a miniature showing the Emperor on horseback in the National Museum of India, New Delhi, in which he wears identical dress, dark green. Green is a Mussulman colour, as is known, and the Emperor was an ardent Muslim.

PLATE XXVII
AURANGZEB 1665

PLATE XXVIII

By 1780 the Mughal Empire was collapsing, and the best painters, having been dismissed from the imperial court, worked at the many Hindu courts; hence our documents originate from the Panjab Hills and Rajasthan, and they possess the extra merit of being a much more popular sort of painting than the artificial and aristocratic miniatures from the Court of Delhi.

Three basic forms of women's dresses exist in this transitional period, and are all illustrated here. The chief lady wears a red skirt, a brown bodice and a diaphanous pale blue veil with gold border and little white flower dots. The veil is not tucked in.

The lady in inset (c) wears a dull mauve frock-like shirt, of Iranian origin *via* the Mughals. This opens in front, is held by a clasp, and under it is a chrome yellow shirt. The veil is now the same colour as the frock. This dress (the *pasvaj*) goes out of fashion almost completely, except in remote areas such as Chamba, or among *pardanashin* women of the Muslim community.

The third fashion is the precursor of the sari. The woman in (b) wears the old blue-striped skirt, with a green bodice, but the *orhni* has become a far more important piece of dress; it is bright brick-red, covering the head, hanging down, tucked into the waistband and gathered in front of the skirt. This is how the sari is still worn in some parts of India, without completely covering the skirt; but the next step, when the head covering also becomes a covering for the skirt, is seen in Plate XXIX.

The men imitate the court fashions. Rama and Lakshmana, Krishna and the heroes of the romances and epics, are all dressed as Mughal courtiers. The Lover in inset (a) could come from Agra; he is the Nayaka in a picture from Kangra, with gold sash, cream-coloured *jama*, matching turban with gold braiding, and trousers in red, with black stripes.

REFERENCES

Archer, *Garhwal Painting* (Faber Gallery, 1954), pl. 5. Archer, *Kangra Painting* (Faber Gallery, 1952), pl. 3, pl. 5, and others. The Raja of Lambagaon's collection, reproduced by *Marg*, in a calendar, illustrating the month of Ashvin.

PLATE XXIX

The birth of the sari. The *dupatta*, or head-kerchief, has now become so long that it falls from the head, is tucked in around the skirt, covering it almost completely, and is gathered in front in thick folds. Note, therefore, that the sari of the 19th and 20th century was not developed out of what had once been called the sari, *viz.* the lower garment, the *dhoti*, the sarong-shaped length of cloth tucked around the waist; but is a lengthening of the headdress, an evolution of the head-covering, the *orhni*, which was not only tucked into the skirt half-heartedly (as it is still done by millions of women in Rajasthan and elsewhere today), but tucked in to such good effect that it now covers the skirt altogether, turning the erstwhile *ghaghra* into a petticoat.

In the Kangra picture the young lady in this Plate has a long enough *orhni* (or sari) to cover her head and to wind it round as a covering for her bodice, to go round the skirt and be thickly folded in front. This is almost the modern sari, with only the small difference that the *orhni* in this Plate is not tucked in *all round* the waistband, and that the lady is not ashamed of shewing small portions of the skirt-petticoat as would be the woman of today. By 1800, this long head-covering is fast spreading in the Panjab Hills and Rajasthan, and by 1820, all over Northern India, the sari is used, from Bombay to Bengal, where early English painters of the period show it as being worn, (though not yet by John Zoffany, who worked in India in 1783-89). It is also noteworthy that the sari used in 1790 is made, just as is the sari in fashion in 1960, of thin material; but where it is thickly gathered, as in front, it is not diaphanous.

REFERENCES

AIP., pl. 152, Randhava, *Kangra Valley Painting*, pl. 4, and many others.

PLATE XXIX
KANGRA, 1790

PLATE XXX

The original miniature painting from which the main figure and the three heads are taken also contains an English officer in a red coat. The Mughal Empire was breathing its last, but luxury continued at the Court of Delhi. The men *à la mode* wore heavy coats, richly laced with gold braiding (unknown in earlier reigns). Here there are two slits in the skirt of the coat on the right and left, with extra lacing, and there is gold braid (lacing) on the shoulders and the upper arm as well as on the sleeve. There is a plastron under the neck, made of different material from the coat, which is now not buttoned over the right chest, but has a large V-shaped opening in front, ending at the sash, with a buttoned-in centre-piece.

A similar dress, of cheaper cotton material, is worn by masses of people. The pedlar in the bottom corner of the opposite Plate is from a 'bazar painting' in Patna, about 1810. He, too, as did so many others at Court, wears a rather flat, almost hat-shaped turban. But others wore many styles of headgear, and a few are illustrated in the Plate.

REFERENCES

With the exception of the pedlar, all the drawings are from a rather large tableau, painted by Sheikh Alam, of an imperial darbar, now in London. (Reproduced in colour in the *Times of India Annual* for 1940). Almost all the figures, over 40, wear baggy trousers, some are with riding boots. The pedlar is from Mrs. Mildred Archer's *Patna Painting* (Royal India Society, London, 1947), pl. 1.

PLATE XXX

DELHI c. 1820

Pedlar, Patna

BIBLIOGRAPHY

Note : This Bibliography could run into dozens of pages, for almost every book and article dealing with Indian sculpture and painting would contain illustrations bearing on the dress of ancient and medieval India. Every *Annual Report* of the Archaeological Survey of India, every number of the *Annual Bibliography of Indian Archaeology* (Kern Institute, Leyden), and most of the *Memoirs* of the Archaeological Survey would be of great use to a student of ancient Indian costume. This Bibliography, therefore, concentrates on the most valuable publications only, exclusively from the point of view of dress in India, and I mark with an asterisk (*) those books that contain much information or outstandingly good pictures in this respect.

ON COSTUME

Brij Bhushan, Jamila. *The Costumes and Textiles of India.* F. Lewis, London, 1958.

*Chandra, Dr. Moti. *Prachin Bharatiya Ves-bhusha* ('Ancient Indian Attire and Ornament', in Hindi). Bharati-Bhandar, Allahabad, 1955.

Fabri, Dr. C.L. 'Ballet Costume in Akbar's Time', *Marg*, VII, 1, Bombay, 1953.

———, 'Two notes on Indian Head-dress', *Journal of the Royal Asiatic Society*, London, July 1931

Ghurye, Prof. G.S. *Bharatanatya and its Costume.* Popular Book Depot, Bombay, 1959.

———, *Indian Costume*, 1957.

*Goetz, Hermann. 'Kostume und Mode an den indischen Fuerstenhofen in der Grossmoghulszeit' ('Costume and Fashion at Indian Princely Courts during the Time of the

Great Mughals', in German) in *Jahrbuch der asiatischen Kunst*, Leipzig, 1924.

ART HISTORY

Bachhofer, L. Von. *Early Indian Sculpture*. Two volumes. New York.

★*Cambridge History of India, The*. Each volume contains a chapter by an authority on the arts of the period, with illustrations. An extra volume under the title *The Indus Civilization*, by Sir Mortimer Wheeler (Cambridge, 1953), gives the latest results on the subject, with pictures.

Chanda, Ramaprasad. *Medieval Indian Sculpture in the British Museum*. Kegan Paul, London, 1950.

★Codrington, K. de B., John Irwin and Basil Gray. *The Art of India and Pakistan*, edited by Sir Leigh Ashton. Faber and Faber, London, 1950.

★Coomaraswamy, A.K. *History of Indian and Indonesian Art*. 1st edition, London, 1927. 2nd edition, London, 1950.

Fabri, C.L. 'Akhnur Terra-cottas', *Marg*, VIII, 2, 1955. The title of this monograph has been erroneously changed. It was correctly titled in the manuscript 'Kashmir Terracottas', for it deals with sculpture found not only at Akhnur but also at Ushkar and Harwan.

———, 'Buddhist Baroque in Kashmir', *Asia*, New York, 1939.

———, 'Frescoes of Ajanta', *Marg*, IX, 1, 1955.

★———, 'Mathura of the Gods', *Marg*, VII, 2, 1954.

★———, 'The Sculpture of the Sun Temple (Konarak) : a study in styles', *Marg*, XII, 1, 1959.

Fischer, O. *Die Kunst Indiens, Chinas und Japans* ('The Art of India, China and Japan', in German) Propylaen-Kunstgeschichte, Berlin, 1928.

★*5000 Jahre Kunst aus Indien*. Catalogue of the Indian Exhibition in Essen; German; also English edition. Essen-Bredeney, 1959.

Goetz, Hermann. *Indien : Fuenf Jahrtausende indischer Kunst*

('Five Thousand Years of Indian Art', in German). Holle-Verlag, Baden-Baden, 1959.

Hackin, J. *La sculpture indienne et tibetaine au Musée Guimet* ('Indian and Tibetan Sculpture in the Musée Guimet', in French).

★Kar, Chintamoni. *Classical Indian Sculpture : 300* B.C. *to 500* A.D. Tiranti, London, 1950.

★Kramrisch, Stella. *The Art of India.* Phaidon, London, 1954.

———, *Grundzuege der indischen Kunst* ('Outlines of Indian Art', in German). Dresden, 1924.

★Rambach, Pierre and Victor de Golish. *The Golden Age of Indian Art : Vth-XIIIth Century.* English edition by Taraporevala, Bombay, 1955.

★Rowland, Benjamin. *The Art and Architecture of India.* The Pelican History of Art. Penguin Books, London, 1953.

Swarup, Shanti. *The Arts and Crafts of India and Pakistan.* Taraporevala, Bombay, 1957.

★Vogel, J.-Ph. 'La Sculpture de Mathura' ('The Sculpture of Mathura', in French), *Art Asiatica*, Paris and Brussels, 1930.

★Yazdani, Dr. Ghulam. *History of the Deccan*, volume I, part VIII : *The Fine Arts* (separately bound). Oxford University Press, 1952.

★Zimmer, Heinrich (completed and edited by Joseph Campbell). *The Art of Indian Asia.* Two volumes. Bollingen Series, XXXIX. Pantheon Books, New York, 1955. These volumes contain more pictures than any other book so far published on the subject.

ON PAINTING

Archer, Mildred. *Patna Painting.* India Society, London, 1947.

★Archer, W.G. *Garhwal Painting.* Faber, London, 1954.

★———, *Indian Painting in the Punjab Hills.* Her Majesty's Stationery Office, London, 1952.

★———, *Kangra Painting.* Faber, London, 1952.

Barrett, Douglas. *Painting of the Deccan : XVI-XVII Century.* Faber, London, 1958.

★Binyon, Lawrence and Sir Thomas Arnold. *Court Painters of the Grand Moguls.* London, 1921.

★Brown, Percy. *Indian Painting under the Mughals.* Oxford, 1924.

★Brown, W. Norman. *A Descriptive and Illustrated Catalogue of Miniature Paintings of the Jain Kalpasutra,* etc. Washington, 1934.

★———, *Manuscript Illustrations of the Uttaradhyayana Sutra.* New Haven, 1941.

★———, *The Story of Kalaka.* Washington, 1933.

Coomaraswamy, Ananda K. *Rajput Painting.* Oxford, 1916.

Dickinson, Eric and Karl Khandalavala. *Kishangarh Painting.* Lalit Kala Akademi, New Delhi, 1959.

Gita-Govinda in Basohli Painting, The. Oxford Book and Stationery Co., New Delhi and Calcutta, 1959.

★Gluck, Heinrich. *Die indischen Miniaturen des Haemzae Romanes* ('The Indian Miniatures of the Hamza Romance', in German). Vienna, 1925.

★Gray, Basil. *Rajput Painting.* Faber, London, 1948.

———, *Treasures of Indian Miniatures.* Cassirer, Oxford, 1951. Contains the same colour plates as Dr Goetz's *The Art and Archaeology of Bikaner State,* Cassirer, Oxford, 1953.

Indian Art through the Ages. Revised edition. Publications Division, Ministry of Information and Broadcasting, Delhi, 1951.

Khandalavala, Karl. *Pahari Miniature Painting.* The New Book Company, Bombay, 1959.

★Kramrisch, Stella. *A Survey of Painting in the Deccan.* India Society, London, 1937.

★Marshall, Sir John, and others. *The Bagh Caves.* London, 1927.

★*Mughal Miniatures.* Notes by Krishnadasa Rai. Lalit Kala Akademi, New Delhi, 1955.

★Singh Madanjeet. *Paintings from Ajanta Caves.* Unesco-New York Graphic Society, New York, 1954.

*Stchoukine, Ivan. *La peinture indienne a l'époque des Grands Moghols* ('Indian Painting at the Time of the Great Mughals', in French). Leroux, Paris, 1929. Though this volume has no colour plates, it is one of the most richly illustrated books on this subject.

*Stooke, Herbert J. and Karl Khandalavala. *The Laud Ragamala Miniatures*. Cassirer, Oxford, 1953.

*Wilkinson, J.V.S. *Mughal Painting*. Faber, London, 1948.

*Yazdani, Ghulam, and others. *Ajanta*. Four volumes of text and four portfolios of photographs. Oxford University Press, 1931-1955.

SERIALS AND PERIODICALS

Apart from the Annual *Reports of the Archaeological Survey of India* and the *Annual Bibliography of Indian Archaeology*. (Kern Institute, Leyden), the following contain much material of importance :

Ancient India. Archaeological Survey of India

Journal of the Indian Society of Oriental Art, Calcutta

Marg, a quarterly magazine, published in Bombay.

Memoirs of the Archaeological Survey of India

INDEX

Adil Shah II : 18.
Agra : 12, 23, 74, 78, 86.
aigrette : 82, 84.
Ajanta : 2, 4, 5, 9, 10, 12, 13, 17, 21, 32, 34, 44, 46, 48.
Akbar, emperor : 24, 70, 72, 74, 78.
Alexandrian, *see* : Greek.
Amaravati : 11, 14, 36, 38.
Anand, Dr. Mulk Raj : 31.
Andhra, State : 6, 11, 25, 60, 66n. See also : Amaravati, Jaggayyapeta, Nagarjunakonda.
anklet : 10, 36, 38, 42, 44, 46, 52, 64, 66.
Archer, Mrs. Mildred : 90n.
Archer, W.G. : 86n.
armlet : 10, 38, 40, 44, 54, 60, 66, 84.
Ashton, Sir Leigh : 31.
Asoka, emperor : 11, 16, 20, 22.
Aurangabad, town : 10.
Aurangzeb, emperor : 76, 84.

Babar, emperor : 23, 68, 72.
Bagh Caves : 5.
baindi, red dot on forehead of women : 44.
Bali, Balinese : 3, 6.
bare upper body : 3–6, 15, 20, 25, 32, 46, 64.
baroque : 1, 22, 48, 50, 52.
Barrett, Douglas : 38n.
beard : 34, 56, 62.
Begram, site, Afghanistan : 42.
belt : 21, 22, 36, 42, 52, 54, 56, 64, 66, and *passim*. *Cp. also* : mekhala, patka.
Belur, temple, Mysore : 58.
Bengal : 54, 88.
Bharata-Natya-Sastra, Sanskrit treatise : 14.
Bharhut, Buddhist monument : 21, 32.
Bihar : 54.
Bijapur, town : 8.
bikinis, very short shorts worn by women : 26.
blanket, wrap=chadar : 12.
blouse, *see* : choli.
Bodhisattva : 40n.
bodice, *see* : choli.
Bombay : 88.
boots : 21, 68. *Cp. Also* : shoes.
bracelet : 10, 34, 38, 40, 42, plate XIV, 60, 66, 72, 84.
breast ornament : 40. *Cp. also*: necklace.
British : 14, 19, 25. *See also* : English.
brocade : 18, 19, 24, 76, 80.
Brown, Percy : 70n.
Brown, W. Norman : 6, 62n.
Buddhist : 2, 12, 14, 18.

Calicut, town in Malabar : 19.
Campbell, Joseph : 31.
Central Asia : 5, 8, 13, 16, 17, 22, 40, 68.
chadar=blanket, wrap : 12, 40.
Chalukya, dynasty : 50.

INDEX

Chamba, State in the Panjab hills : 86.
Chandra, Dr. Moti : 2, 7, 16, 17.
Chandragupta Maurya, emperor : 11.
China, Chinese : 16, 17, 76.
Chingleput, Madras : 64n.
Chola queen : 4, 11, 64, plate XVII.
choli=bodice, blouse : 6, 10, 13, 21, 23, 62, 64, 74, 86, 88.
coat : 7, 11, 12, 14, 25, 68, 70, 76, 84, 90. *See also* : jama, shirt.
coat-of-mail : 11, 21.
Codrington, K. de B.: 31.
collar : 82
colour, in dress, in textiles : 17, 18, 20, 24, 32, 44, 48, 58, 62, 64, 68, 74, 78, 82.
'corkscrew' hair curls : 46.
cotton : 16, 90, and *passim*.
crown : 10, 50, 66.
curls of hair : 46, 48n.

Dacca, town in Bengal : 19.
dagger : *see* : side arms.
dancer, dancing girl : 5, 10, 11, 56, 58, 80. Plate XIV.
Dasavatara temple, *see* : Deogarh.
Deccan, part of Andhra State : 18, 23, 24, 25, 52, 58n, 60, 78. *See also* : Andhra, Ajanta.
Delhi : 12, 23, 74, 78, 86, plate XXX, 90.
Deogarh, U.P.: 8, 46n.
dhoti, length of cloth falling from waist : 7, 11, 17, 22, 25, 32, 36, 40, 46, 48, 52, 54, 60, 88. *See also* : sari.
diadem : 10, 44, 50, 58. *See also* : crown.
Dickens, Charles : 7.
dinner jacket : 25.
dirk, *see* : side arms.

Draupadi, heroine in the *Mahabharata* : 6.
dupatta = head-kerchief : 7, 21, 23, 24, 25, 32, 58, 88. *See* : orhni.
Durga, goddess : 5.
Dutch : 19.
dvarapala=doorkeeper : 17.

Earrings : 10, 34, 42, 50, 52, 58, 60, 66.
East India Company : 25.
Edward VII, king : 7.
Egyptians : 21.
Ellura, Ellora, caves in Andhra : 50.
English : 19, 25, 90.
Essen, Germany, exhibition of Indian art : 66n.

Fabri, Dr Charles : 2, 14, 32n, 44n, 48n.
Far East : 21.
feathers : 76.
finger rings : 84.
flax : 18.
foreigners, foreign : 3, 5, 9, 11, 13, 17, 20, 23, 40, 42, 46.
Foucher, Prof. Alfred : 40n.
French : 19.
frock : 7, 23, 72, 86.

Gandhara, ancient kingdom in the Panjab and the Kabul valley : 2, 11, 17, 18, 23, 40.
ghaghra=skirt : 13, 18, 23, 24, 62, 74, 86, 88.
Goetz, Dr Hermann : 23.
gown : 7
Gray, Basil : 8, 31, 74n.
Greek, Greco-Roman, Greece : 4, 5, 11, 12, 16, 21, 23, 34, 42, 46, 56.

INDEX

Gujarat, State, miniatures : 6, 9, 17, 18, 58, 62, 64.
Gupta, dynasty, 320–495 A.D., and the style of that time : 44, 46n.
Gwalior, Rajasthan: 54n.

Hair, hair style, hair-dress : 22, 46, 48, 50, 52, 54, 56, 64, 66.
Halebid, temple in Mysore : 60.
'halo' style coiffure : 48, 52.
Harappa, prehistoric site, and culture first found there : 12.
hat : 7, 90.
Hawaiian bush shirt : 25.
head-dress, head covering : 42, 44. See also : hair, turban.
head-kerchief, see : dupatta, orhni, scarf.
hetaera, Greek courtesan, harlot : 56.
Hindu : 12, 18, 23, 24, 74, 86, and passim.
Humayun, emperor : 23, 68, 72.
Huns : 8.
Hyderabad, Andhra : 66n.

Iran, see : Persia.
Irwin, John : 31.
Islam, Muslim : 11, 12, 18, 22–26, 60ff, 74, 84, 86.

Jaggayyapeta, site in Andhra : 11.
Jahangir, emperor : 24, 70, 76, 78, 80.
jama = Mughal buttoned coat : 14, 24, 25, 26, 74, 86.
jatakas, Buddhist tales of morality : 2.
jeans : 23, 26.
jerkin : 80.
jewellery : 10, 32, 36, 40, 42, 44, 46, 48, 50, 52, 54, 56, 58, 82, 84.
jodhpurs, type of breeches, tight from the knee down : 24.
Julius Caesar : 14.

Kabul : 17, 42.
Kalidasa : 14. *See also* : *Sakuntala*.
kamarband = cummerbund, kind of waist belt : 24, 34.
kamiz=kind of shirt : 23.
Kangra, part of the Panjab hill region : 18, 86, plate XXIX, 88. *See also* : Panjab.
Karle Caves, near Bombay : 36.
Kathakali, dance drama of Kerala : 14.
kaunakes = 'woollen cloth made of a plant' : 16.
Kerala : 6, 25, 60.
Khajuraho, in Madhya Pradesh : 10, 58.
Khan Alam : 80.
Khusrau, prince : 80.
Kramrisch, Stella : 31, 32n, 34n, 36n, 38n, 46n, 52n, 56n, 58n.
Krishna, the cowherd-god : 12, 13, 24, 74n, 86.
kshatriya=member of the princely and warrior caste : 56.
kula=conical skull cap of Muslims round which turban is wound : 68, 72.
Kumbakonam, town, Madras : 56.
Kushana, Central Asian tribe, settled in Northern India : 17, 36n.

Lahore : 24, 74.
Lakshmana, brother of Rama : 86.
Lambagaon, Raja of : 86n.
Laud, Bishop : 78.
Levant trade : 19.
linen : 18.

literary references : 7, 24.
Little Clay Cart, The, Sanskrit play : 15.

Madras : 60.
Mahabharata : 7, 23.
Mahendravarman, king : 4, 50, plate X.
mail-coat, see : coat-of-mail.
mala=garland : 34.
Malwa, part of Rajasthan : 18.
Mamallapuram (*vulgo* : Mahabalipuram), near Madras : 50.
mannerism : 48.
Mathura, town in U.P. : 2, 11, 36, 40, 42.
mekhala=metal girdle : 23, 32, 36.
men-at-arms, see : soldier.
mendicant : 34.
Mesopotamia : 16, 19.
military, see : soldier.
Mohenjo-daro, prehistoric site in Sindh : 12, 16.
moirée=shot silk : 48.
Mosul, town in Mesopotamia : 19.
moustaches : 34.
Mudra-rakshasa, Sanskrit play : 5.
Mughal, Mughal court : 1, 2, 12, 13, 18, 21, 23, 86, 90.
Muslim, see : Islam, Mughal.
muslin : 19, 34, 48, 78, 80.
Mysore : 8.

Nagarjunakonda, ancient site in Andhra : 11, 13, 38.
Nayika-Nayaka = 'Hero' and 'Heroine', love scenes in literature and painting : 23, 74, 86.
necklace : 10, plate III, 40, 42, 54, 56, 58, 60, 84.
nurse's cap : 46.
nylon : 26.

Officer : 34, *see also* : soldier.
orhni=head-kerchief : 7, 13, 18, 23, 25, 26, 32, 62, 72, 74, 78, 86, 88.
Cp. : dupatta.
Orissa, Oriyas : 6, 11, 58, 64, plate XII, plate XIV.
Orissi Dance : 58.

Pagri=turban. See : turban.
Pahari, Pahari painting. See : Panjab.
Paharpur, ancient site in Bengal : 54.
pai-jamas=trousers : 24, 70.
Palestine : 5.
Panini, Sanskrit grammarian : 16.
Panjab, Panjabi Hill (Pahari) painting : 8, 12, 13, 18, 21, 22, 23, 40, 86, 88.
pardanashin = women in veil : 86.
Parvati, goddess : 60.
pasvaj, also spelt, incorrectly, peshwas = frock-like garment of women : 21, 22, 23, 86.
Pathan : 40
patka=sash : 14, 24, 72, 74, 76, 78, 80, 82, 92.
Patna, Bihar : 90.
Pattadakal, temple city in Mysore : 50.
peplum, peplos, Greek dress: 11, 23, 42.
Persia, Persians, Iran, Iranians : 13, 21, 22, 42, 62, 86.
pesh-was, see : pasvaj.
petticoat : 7, 25, 88.
Pickwick, Mr : 7.
plastron : 90.
pompom : 70, 72, 74, 78.
Portuguese : 19, 25.

Ragamala, Sanskrit=garland of musical themes : 78.

Rajasthan : 6, 8, 12, 18, 24, 25, 54, 64, 74, 78, 86, 88.
Rajmahal, Bihar : 54n.
Rajput : 14, 18, 23, 24. *See also* : Rajasthan.
Rama : 86.
Ramayana : 23, 60.
Rambach, Pierre, and Victor de Golish : 48n, 50n, 52n, 58n.
Randhava, M.S. : 88 n.
repoussé : 10.
riding boots, *see* : boots.
ring, *see* : finger ring.
rococo : 22, 56, 58, 60, 64.
Roman, Rome, Roman empire : 5, 11, 16, 18, 21. *See also* : Greek.
Rowland, Benjamin : 31, 32n, 34n, 40n, 42n, 60n, 62n.
'rumi', coming from 'Rum', the Roman Empire : 5.

Sacred thread, *see* : yajnopavita.
Sakuntala, heroine of Kalidasa's Sanskrit drama : 9, 15.
Sanchi, ancient site in U.P. : 13, 22.
sandals : 12, 34, 40.
Sarguja, in Madhya Pradesh : 36n.
sari : 6-9, 11, 24, 42, 78, 86n, 88.
sarong : 7, 32, 52, 54, 88. *See also* : dhoti.
'Sasanian ribbon' : 42.
sash : *passim*. *See also* : patka, belt.
scarf : 5, 20, 21, 34, 46, 48, 54, 56, 58, 62, 64. *Cp*. orhni, dupatta.
Scythian : 5.
Seleucus, emperor : 11.
Serindia : 16.
sewn garment : 20, 22, 23, 42, 48.
silk : 16-19, 24, 48, 76, 80, 84.
Shahjehan, emperor : 82.
Shakespeare : 14.
shalvar=baggy trousers : 23.
shaving : 34.

shawl, *see* : scarf.
Sheikh Alam : 90n.
shirt : 25, 34, 68, 72, 74, 86. *See also* : boots, sandals.
shorts : 25.
side-arm (sword, dagger, dirk) : 21, 52, 66, 70, 72.
Sigiriya, site in Ceylon : 44.
simul silk : 17.
Singh, Madanjeet : 48n.
Sita, heroine of the *Ramayana*: 9, 60.
skirt, *see* : ghaghra.
soldier, military : 11, 20, 21, 34, 52, 68.
South India : 2, 6, 9, 11, 12, 25, 36, 38, 60, 64, 66, 78.
Spanish : 19.
stage, theatre : 9-10, 15-16.
Stchoukine, Ivan : 68n, 70n, 76n, 80n, 82n, 84n.
Stein, Sir Aurel : 17.
Stooke, Herbert J., and Karl Khandalavala : 78n.
sword, *see* : side-arm.
Syria : 5.

Tahmad=single sheet of cloth, hanging from waist, worn mainly by Muslims : 46.
Takla Makan desert in Central Asia : 16.
Tamil land, *see* : South India, Madras.
Tamil poetry : 66.
tang pai-jamas=tight trousers, leggings : 24.
Tanjore, Madras : 58n.
tassel : 52, 54, 58, 72, 74, 78.
Taxila, in Gandhara : 13.
theatre, *see* : stage.
'three-piece-dress' : 14, 19, 24, 74, 78.
Timon of Athens : 14.

Timurid, of the dynasty of Timur-leng (Tamberlane) : 23, 24, 68ff. *See also* : Mughal.
Tippu Sultan : 8.
trousers : 14, 23, 26, 60, 72, 76, 80, 82, 86. *See also* : pai-jama, shalvar, tang pai-jama.
turban : 12, 21, 23, 32, 34, 36, 38, 40, 42, 68, 72, 76, 78, 82, 84, 86, 88.
turra=fan-shaped end of turban cloth : 40.

Uniform : 21, 68, 72.

Vats, M.S. : 46n.
veil, *see* : orhni, dupatta, scarf.
velvet : 18-19.
Vogel, J. Ph. : 40n.
vrikshaka = dryad, wood nymph : 32.

Warangal, in Andhra : 60.
western servants, *see* : foreigner.
'wig' style head-dress : 46.
Wilkinson, J.V.S. : 72n.
Wolseley, Cardinal : 7.

Yajnopavita=sacred thread : 14, 50, 52, 54, 60, 66.
yaksha, yakshi(ni) = spirits, gods of forests and waters, nymphs, dryads, fauns : 32.
Yavanika='Ionian' girl, *i.e.* from Western Asia : 5, 46.
Yazdani, Ghulam : 31, 32n, 44n, 46n, 48n.

Zimmer, Heinrich : 31, 32n, 34n, 36n, 38n, 40n, 48n, 50n, 54n, 56n, 58n, 60n.
Zoffany, John, English painter of Austrian origin : 88.

NOTES

The letter n after a page number refers to the Reference footnotes on the descriptive pages opposite plates. Words and names in the List of Plates have not been indexed. *Italics* are titles of books etc.